Minecraft® Recipes

FOR DUMMIES®

A Wiley Brand

Portable Edition

by Jesse Stay and
Thomas Stay

D1497695

FOR DUMMIES®
A Wiley Brand

Minecraft® Recipes For Dummies® Portable Edition

Published by **John Wiley & Sons, Inc.,** 111 River Street, Hoboken, NJ 07030-5774, www.wiley.com

Copyright © 2015 by John Wiley & Sons, Inc., Hoboken, New Jersey

Published simultaneously in Canada

Contents at a Glance

Table of Contents

Chapter 4: Advancing through Engineering 69

Introduction

*I*f you're reading this book there's a good chance you're one of two people – a parent, wanting to learn more about what your kids are doing in Minecraft, or a teen or pre-teen wanting to have a quick reference to learn every little recipe you can get your hands on within the vast world of Minecraft. This book is for both of you!

Minecraft, or as Jesse calls it, "Virtual LEGOs," are the building blocks of the new generation. From geology to construction to mining to gardening, and even electricity, programming, and logic, Minecraft will teach you (if you're in the pre-teen crowd), or your children (if you're the parent) all sorts of things as you explore this mystical universe.

Minecraft is all about exploring. The more you explore, the more you discover. It's our hope that as you explore this book, you'll also discover many new things you can try in the incredible world of Minecraft!

About This Book

From Jesse (Thomas's Dad):

When I was 10 years old I took a programming course in the summer that changed my life. I was enamored by the ability to make things on the screen, and watch them perform, as I told them to perform. I started reading articles in the *3-2-1 Contact* magazine I got every month and trying out the programming examples I learned in the back, adapting, learning, and soon creating my own things.

This type of learning has gone away in our current school system and society. We just expect our kids to gain programming knowledge, and there are not many places on computers for them to explore like I had growing up. It wasn't until my kids started to play Minecraft that I started to see this environment of exploration come back into mine, and my kids', life.

When I started building the concepts of this book, I realized how great a family activity the game of Minecraft is. The truth is, my son Thomas and my other sons are really the experts, and I'm here to learn from them, so I approached the book in this same manner. In fact I let Thomas write most of the book — yes, this book was written by a 12 year old just like you, your siblings, or even your children (if you're an adult). Then, I would review his material, make sure you could understand it, and added any missing content I felt you might be interested in. Sometimes even his younger brothers Joseph and JJ, would pitch in a screenshot or a tip.

In this book, we assume you may have a little knowledge of Minecraft (perhaps through *Minecraft For Dummies*), but need a good reference on what you can do in Minecraft, and what types of things you need to gather to advance in the game. This book serves as a reference to help you start building, and once you know how to build, you can then focus on the exploring, the true essence of Minecraft.

This book is a reference. You should be able to pick it up, and sift from chapter to chapter and not even in order, and you'll still be able to learn plenty. There is no need to read each chapter in order (but if you do, that's great too!).

Minecraft is constantly updating. There will likely be new recipes, potions, and other types of creations that get released perhaps even before this goes to print. We did our best to include as many as we can in this book, but there will certainly be more!

From Thomas:

In this book, the knowledge that you get is nothing like anything you've ever seen before. When I started out on Minecraft, I knew a lot about the game, but I didn't know any of the recipes, much less what the blocks could do. I didn't know most of the enchantments, or much about brewing potions. This book takes a player with average or beginner experience, just like a 12-year-old me, and leads that guy or girl to a much higher level in the game. Most people don't know a lot of things in Minecraft when they first get started. This book teaches you how to get there. As you read this, I'll take you along the same journey I did.

To stay up-to-date on updates, be sure to follow the Minecraft Wiki at http://minecraft.gamepedia.com. We will also be posting updates on Facebook at http://facebook.com/minecraftrecipes, and even our YouTube channel at http://youtube.com/minecraftrecipesfd.

Foolish Assumptions

We'd rather not assume anything. But because there are so many of you, we have to assume a few things! These are the things you should probably have available, or be familiar with as you go throughout this book:

- You have a computer or a mobile device (chances are most of you are playing Minecraft on a mobile device through Minecraft PE)
- You know basic skills of accessing the Internet.
- If using the PC version, your computer can download and run Java programs.
- You have a basic understanding of making your way around Minecraft.

Icons Used in This Book

For your convenience, we've placed icons throughout the margins to help you understand more about the content we're sharing. These are the common icons and how we use them:

If we have a tip to share in addition to the content you're reading, you see this icon.

When we present information you'll want to keep top of mind, this icon appears in the margin next to that information.

This is the stuff you should pay attention to – don't skip it! Something will go wrong if you don't heed the advice here.

Perhaps for the more geeky, or just those that like to learn, this will take you to the next level, and show you how to learn more than what this book was intended for.

Conventions Used in This Book

Throughout the book, you'll see numbered steps, bullet lists, screen shots, as well as little icons signifying different ingredients for recipes. You may also see web addresses in monotype font that look like this:

```
http://minecraft.gamepedia.com
```

Where to Go from Here

This is only the beginning! Remember: the end game is not necessarily the end! Take the things you learn here and explore. Go check out redstone and explore new ways to build advanced circuitry and logic. Build your own worlds! Build a farm! Make your own mods. Quite literally, the world is at your fingertips in Minecraft!

If you really want to take it to another level, we mentioned in the earlier section, "About This Book," the Minecraft wiki. We also suggest the Facebook Page (`http://facebook.com/minecraftrecipes`) and YouTube channel (`http://youtube.com/minecraftrecipesfd`) where we'll post regular updates of current and new recipe ideas in Minecraft. Come join us (Thomas and sometimes his younger brothers and Jesse) and say hi!

1

Getting Started with Recipes

In This Chapter

- Finding, stocking, and using your inventory
- Crafting items you need for the first day and night
- Knowing the difference between shape and shapeless crafting
- Crafting some basic tools

*M*inecraft, as its name implies, is about, well, crafting. Minecraft has roughly 180 crafting recipes (and many more in the works), ranging from tools to foods and from household items to magical potions and more. Learning how to craft from essential items to more elaborate redstone recipes helps you survive early in the game and then create a wealthy empire filled with useful and luxury items.

After you create a new world in Minecraft, the first order of business is to survive the first night. A Minecraft day lasts for 20 minutes; you experience 10-minute daytimes and 3 minutes total of sunrise and sunset, during which you can prepare for the 7-minute nights, when dangerous monsters spawn in the darkness.

In this chapter, you find out how the inventory works and how to craft basic items that can help you survive the first Minecraft day. You also see how these items enable you to use increasingly sophisticated materials and craft increasingly complex items.

Devising a Game Plan

After your avatar appears, you need to find a living space with some trees and a suitable (usually flat) area for building.

Always locate trees when starting a game, because you use wooden materials to craft most of the items you need. To survive the first night, craft these elements:

- ✔ Crafting table (also known as a workbench), used for building
- ✔ Storage chest
- ✔ Shelter with a door

You can also craft useful but non-essential items for the first night:

- ✔ Wooden and stone tools
- ✔ Torches
- ✔ Furnace
- ✔ Bed

Later sections in this chapter explain how to craft these items.

When you start creating your own world, you may discover that the sun is setting too fast for you to finish preparing for night. If that's the case, you can press Esc to open the Pause menu and choose Options⊏⊃Difficulty repeatedly until it reads `Difficulty: Peaceful`. This option makes the world much safer and causes your health to regenerate.

Using the Inventory

Before you start gathering materials and crafting items, you should know how to manage the Inventory screen. The 9 squares at the bottom of the game screen display items you've obtained. For example, if you break a block such as wood or dirt, an item pops out that is automatically picked up, causing it to appear in one of the inventory squares. The row of squares at the bottom of the game screen represents a quarter of the inventory.

To see the entire inventory, as shown in Figure 1-1, press E.

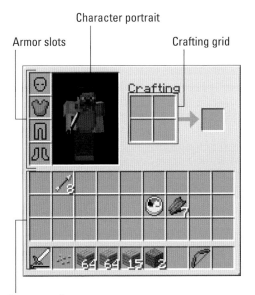

Character portrait

Armor slots   Crafting grid

Inventory slots

Figure 1-1: The Inventory screen.

You should be familiar with these four components of the inventory:

- **Inventory slots:** The 4 rows of squares at the bottom of the screen, where you see your items. You select the items in the bottom row outside the Inventory screen with the 1–9 keys on the keyboard.

- **Crafting grid:** A 2-by-2 square, followed by an arrow pointing toward another square to the right. When you want to craft basic items, such as torches or mushroom stew, place the ingredients on the grid to make the result appear on the other side of the arrow. After you create a crafting table, the crafting grid expands to a 3-by-3 grid.

- **Character portrait:** A small screen showing what your character looks like now. This portrait can change when your character sits or sleeps, wears armor, gets hit by arrows, drinks invisibility potions, catches fire, and more.

↙ **Armor slots:** The four squares in the upper left corner, representing a helmet, a suit, leggings, and boots. When you obtain armor later in the game, you can place it in these slots; Shift-clicking a piece of armor automatically equips it in the corresponding slot. See Chapter 3 for more information about armor.

Crafting in other platforms

Crafting is quite limited and extremely simplified in the Pocket Edition (PE) version of Minecraft. The Inventory screen groups items into these categories:

↙ Blocks

↙ Tools

↙ Food and armor

↙ Decorative Items

To craft, you gather the ingredients you need in order to create the item. Then you simply click on the item you want to create and the items are deducted from the inventory (assuming that you have the correct ingredients). Only a few items are craftable in the PE version and there's no crafting in Creative mode. The inventory display in the Pocket Edition looks like the one shown in the sidebar figure.

Console versions, such as Xbox 360 and PS4, blend the PC (desktop) and PE inventory and crafting processes using a grid format (like PC) but doesn't require that the ingredients be placed in any specific order.

The PE crafting system is called MATTIS, which stands for Minecraft Advanced Touch Technology Interface System.

Because most items are *stackable,* several similar items such as wooden planks or steak can share the same inventory slot; an item may have a white number next to it in the inventory, indicating how many you have. Most stackable items cannot exceed a stack of 64 items — you can fit as many as 64 items into one space. Tools, weapons, and armor do not stack, and some items, such as ender pearls or snowballs, cannot exceed a stack of 16 items.

Manipulating the Inventory

While viewing the full inventory, you can use these basic commands for manipulating items in the inventory:

- **Pick up the items in an inventory square.** Click a square in the inventory to pick up the items there.

- **Pick up half of the items in an inventory square.** Right-click a square in the inventory to pick up half (rounded up) of the items there.

- **Place all items you're holding.** While holding an item or a stack of items, click an empty square to place the item(s) there.

- **Place a single item that you're holding.** While holding a stack of items, right-click an empty square to place *one* item there. The rest remain on the cursor. Right-click several times to place several items.

In addition, while holding an item, you can click outside the Inventory screen to drop the item on the ground. While outside the Inventory screen, you can press the 1–9 keys to select an item from the bottom row of the inventory and then press Q to drop it. If you press the Q key with a stack of items, only one item is thrown.

If you're just starting out with Minecraft, break nearby blocks (as described in the section "Harvesting trees with your fists," later in this chapter) and move them around in the inventory to become familiar with the way the inventory works.

Setting Up for Your First Night

Before nightfall on your first night, you need to complete a few tasks. Start with the essentials, which we discuss in detail in this section:

- **Harvest trees.** Then you can craft wooden planks.
- **Build a crafting table.** It starts off your production of useful items.
- **Build a chest.** Storing items in the chest keeps your items from being lost.
- **Construct a shelter and a door.** The shelter keeps *you* safe from being attacked.

Harvesting trees with your fists

Start the crafting process by chopping down nearby trees. Everything you need in order to build your shelter requires some form of wood, and the most efficient way to get it is to harvest trees. Look for a place with a good number of trees. (If you're too far away from any plants, you may want to create a new world.)

To start, chop down a couple of trees, which are made of wood blocks and leaf blocks. To break a block from the tree, follow these steps:

1. **Walk up to a tree.**

2. **Using the mouse, position the crosshair over a block in the tree.**

3. **Click and hold the left mouse button to start punching the block until it breaks.**

4. **Collect the item that appears.**

   The item should come directly to you, but if you're too far away, just walk up to the item to collect it. The resource is added to the inventory at the bottom of the screen.

Ignore the leaves on the tree for now because they decay naturally with nothing supporting them. Destroyed leaf blocks sometimes give sapling items, which you don't need for crafting the essential items covered in this chapter, but are needed for other recipes you'll discover as you progress through the game.

Creating wooden planks

The wooden plank is one of the most useful items in the game and is the essential ingredient in many recipes, including simple items such as a bed, chest, ax, and sword. Wooden planks can also let you build complex items such as tripwire hooks or pistons. Wooden planks are helpful building blocks: Trees are in abundance, so planks are easy to create.

For now, though, follow these steps to use the wood blocks you've gathered by harvesting trees (as described in the earlier section "Harvesting trees with your fists") to produce wooden planks:

1. **Press E to display the Inventory screen.**

2. **Click a square containing wood blocks to pick them up, and then click an empty square in the crafting grid to place them there.**

   Four wooden planks appear next to the grid, as shown in Figure 1-2.

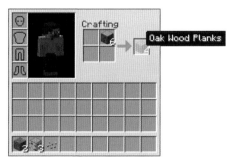

Figure 1-2: Crafting planks.

3. **Click the square that contains the planks.**

   One wood block disappears, but 4 wooden planks appear at the location of the mouse cursor.

4. **Click the square that contains the planks a few more times to pick up all the planks you can, or Shift-click to send all planks directly to the inventory.**

You can use these planks as building blocks or use them to build a crafting table and chest.

Building the crafting table

Your avatar's crafting grid is a 2-x-2 square (refer to Figure 1-2); however, many items you need to survive require a 3-x-3 grid to craft. To unlock this larger grid, you build a crafting table. Follow these steps to build a crafting table, or workbench:

1. **Press E to open the Inventory screen.**

2. **Click a square containing the planks, and then right-click each square in the crafting grid to place one plank in each box of the crafting grid.**

   A crafting table appears on the right, as shown in Figure 1-3.

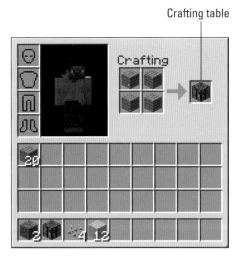

Figure 1-3: The crafting table.

3. **Click the crafting table to pick it up, and then click a square in the bottom row of the inventory to place the table there.**

You can access items outside the Inventory screen only if they're on the bottom row. This row is always displayed at the bottom of the game screen.

4. **Press E or Esc to close the inventory.**

5. **Use the 1–9 keys or the scroll wheel to select the crafting table.**

A thick, white outline appears around the crafting table.

You can use either the number keys or the scroll wheel to select items from the bottom row of the inventory. Place the most useful items in the slots you can quickly access.

6. **Right-click a nearby surface to place the crafting table there.**

Right-click the crafting table to view a screen similar to the inventory, with an expanded crafting grid. You use this grid for all the crafting recipes in the game, including the chest, described in the section "Storing items in a chest."

Storing items in a chest

You can place the chest, which is a storage unit, in your world and fill it with items. The benefit is that you drop all items when your avatar dies, but *not* the items in your storage chests.

The *chest* is a useful item that's used to store other blocks and items. It has 27 slots, and each slot can hold a stack (a stack of cobblestone is 64; eggs, 16; and tools such as swords, 1) of 1 item or block. Putting 2 chests next to each other makes a double chest, holding twice as many slots, or 54 slots in all.

As the game progresses, it's impossible to hold all necessary items in the inventory. Using a chest, you can collect and store whatever you'll need in the future. The texture is complex, giving it the feel of a real-life chest. A special property of chests is that they let light pass through them, allowing items such as plants to continue to grow, and they're smaller than full-size blocks (for example, wooden planks).

To craft a chest, place 8 wooden planks in a circle inside the crafting table grid, leaving 1 slot in the middle (see Figure 1-4). Eight wooden planks get you 1 chest. Now you'll never run out of inventory.

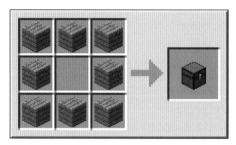

Figure 1-4: Building a chest for storing inventory.

If you right-click the storage chest, you can view an extra grid of squares that's almost as large as the inventory. Placing items into these slots stores them for safekeeping. You can also Shift-click items to sort them from the inventory into the chest, and vice versa. Always keep most of your valuables in storage when you're first starting out. As you become more comfortable playing the game, you can carry more items with you, just in case.

Do not place a block directly above a chest, or else it won't open.

For more efficiency, place a second chest next to the first one to create an elongated chest, which stores twice as many stacks in the same place.

Erecting a shelter and door

Wandering around in the open usually isn't a problem during the day, but your environment becomes much more dangerous at night. If your daytime minutes are waning and you don't feel ready to fight back (which is probably true on your first day), you need shelter. By placing many of the blocks you've gathered, you can build shelters, houses, and other structures.

As you gain experience, you can invent your own architectural strategies. To build a basic shelter for now, follow these steps:

1. **Find a good building spot.**

   Flat spots are the easiest to build on, but you can find any spot that you think is feasible for a house to fit. Remember that you can break and replace dirt, sand, and other blocks to flatten a rough area.

2. **Select a block in the inventory with the 1–9 keys, and then right-click a nearby surface to place it there. Place several blocks in a comfortably sized outline for your base of operations, as shown in Figure 1-5.**

Figure 1-5: Starting your base.

Usually, the frame is a rectangle made of wooden planks, but you can collect blocks such as dirt and use them for building in a pinch. You also need a door, so you can leave one block out of the rectangle to make room for it. You can also build the rectangle around the crafting table and chest so that you can work from inside your home.

3. **Place a second layer of blocks on top of the first layer.**

   A structure that's two blocks tall is sufficient to keep most monsters at bay.

   Eventually, you'll need a roof on your structure. So you will need to make your structure three blocks tall with the third layer filled in, because spiders can get inside without a roof. The roof can also be in a checkerboard pattern, with one block filled in and the next one not and so on to save blocks and keep spiders out.

To place a block beneath you, jump into the air while right-clicking and looking straight down. This popular method for building and scaffolding is referred to as *pillar jumping*. If you repeat this strategy, you can effectively rise upward on a pillar of blocks, which is useful for building taller structures.

Next, craft a door so that you have a simple way to enter and exit the shelter. The door is just a door, but when it's closed, it provides a barrier from mobs, including zombies (except when you're in hard mode). Right-clicking a door opens and closes it. It can be placed only on solid blocks. The door is 2 blocks high, and its texture for the lower half is simple, whereas its upper half has 4 windows that you can look through.

To craft a door, place 6 wooden planks in a vertical row on the crafting table, yielding 3 wooden doors (see Figure 1-6).

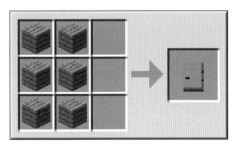

Figure 1-6: Crafting a door.

Here's how to install the door in the inventory to your shelter:

1. **Move the door to the bottom row of the inventory.**

2. **Place the door in the wall of your shelter by right-clicking the ground where you want it.**

   You may have to break open part of the shelter wall to fit the door.

3. **Right-click the door to open (and close) it.**

When you place a door in front of you, the door is positioned to open away from you when you right-click it. Usually, a door is placed from the outside of a building so that it opens toward the inside.

Figure 1-7 shows a finished shelter with a door.

Figure 1-7: Crafting a door and finishing the shelter.

That's it — generally, a basic shelter can ensure your safety for the night.

Getting through the night on a bed

The bed has a unique function in the game, built to help you pass the night without having to wait or defend yourself against mobs and other monsters. You can sleep only at night (which can be confusing at times, and you may want to craft a clock to help with that – see the section in Chapter 3 about mining ore). However, you cannot use your bed when there are monsters nearby (the game will tell you this).

Though a bed is one of the first items a player crafts to further the game, it cannot be that player's only defense. The bed occupies the space of 2 blocks. The texture looks like a tidy bed. To craft, on the crafting table, you put 3 wool on top and 3 wooden planks on the bottom to produce 1 bed (see Figure 1-8).

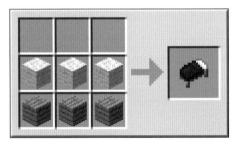

Figure 1-8: Building a bed on the crafting table grid.

To collect wool, you can shear or kill sheep. Because sheep provide no food, many players craft shears as soon as the game allows. To craft your own shears, see the section in Chapter 3 about building utensils.

Shape Crafting versus Shapeless Crafting

If you've read the first half of this chapter and you've crafted wooden planks and a crafting table, you already know generally how to craft. Give yourself a pat on the back. But moving forward, you should know that Minecraft has two types of crafting recipes. The crafting table introduces these two types of recipes:

✔ **Shape:** Every ingredient should go in the exact place specified on the crafting grid for the recipe to work.

✔ **Shapeless:** The placement of items doesn't matter. You can place them willy-nilly.

Crafting Tools

One thing that distinguishes us as humans is our ability to create tools! Minecraft is just like real life in that manner. In order to advance through the game, you need to build tools to help you harvest, mine, and craft items. Knowing what tools are available, and how to use those tools, gives you a critical advantage in playing the game.

Starting with a stick

You use a stick to make tools and ladders and all sorts of other items. A stick is an item, which means that you can't place it in your Minecraft world.

You craft sticks four at a time. To create 4 sticks, place 2 wooden planks on the crafting table, as shown in Figure 1-9.

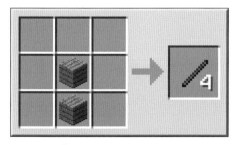

Figure 1-9: Building a stick that you can use to create other tools.

Lighting the way with a torch

The *torch* is a common block that's used to light up areas. Placing it in your Minecraft world lights up dark areas, such as caves and houses. Many types of mobs and other monsters are afraid of light and will avoid the light of a torch.

Cutting stone with the stonecutter in Minecraft PE

Minecraft, Pocket Edition (PE) — the edition for smartphones and tablet devices, such as the iPhone or iPad — works a little differently from the desktop version. As we mention throughout this chapter, to put it simply for now, you don't necessarily "craft" items in the Pocket Edition.

In Minecraft PE, you mine the ingredients you need, and a separate screen lists the items you can create when you have those ingredients. For example, when you have the ingredients to make a crafting table and you then make one, more items appear that you can craft by simply gathering more ingredients and selecting the crafting table.

One major difference in Minecraft PE is that you can't make certain types of items on the crafting table, as you normally can do in the desktop version. Instead, you need to gather the ingredients for a stonecutter and craft it.

After you create the stonecutter, you can make items such as stone slabs that require you first to cut stone. As you place items into the stonecutter, it turns specified items into something else (such as a stone slab or brick slab). This is where you cut (or create) bricks in Minecraft PE.

The texture of the stonecutter is similar to that of the furnace, but the stonecutter has a blade at the top, a blade and hammer on one side, and no holes. You craft it by having 4 cobblestone and clicking the stonecutter button. The sidebar figure shows the screen on which you craft the stonecutter in Minecraft PE. Crafting it gives you 1 stonecutter.

A torch is smaller than a full block. It has different textures, depending on whether it's on the ground or on a wall. On the ground, the bottom looks like wood and the top looks like a flame. On the wall, it's the same, but slanted.

To craft a torch, you need 1 stick and 1 coal or charcoal. Place them on the crafting table on top of each other, as shown in Figure 1-10. Crafting gives you 4 torches.

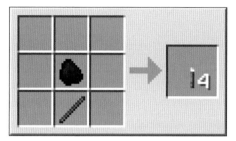

Figure 1-10: Crafting a torch with coal and a stick.

Mining stone and ore with a pickaxe

The *pickaxe* is a tool in Minecraft to collect blocks, such as cobblestone, iron ore, coal ore, and much more.

Of the different tiers, wooden is the lowest and diamond is the highest. To craft a pickaxe, place 2 sticks vertically in the middle of the crafting table, and at the top place 3 of the block tier, as shown in Figure 1-11. (For a wooden pickaxe, use wooden planks, for example.) Crafting this item gives you 1 pickaxe.

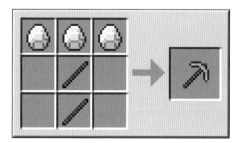

Figure 1-11: Building a pickaxe in the crafting grid.

From lowest to highest, the tiers are wood, stone, iron, gold, and diamond. See Table 1-1 for details about how to create each type of pickaxe and what each pickaxe can do.

Table 1-1		Crafting Pickaxes	
Pickaxe	*Type*	*Craft with This Item. . . and 2 Sticks*	*Use It to Mine This Item*
⛏	Wood	Wooden plank	Coal ore
⛏	Stone	Cobblestone	Coal or iron ore
⛏	Iron	Iron ingot	Coal or iron ore, diamonds
⛏	Gold	Gold ingot	Coal ore
⛏	Diamond	Diamond	Coal or iron ore, diamonds, obsidian

A gold pickaxe has the least amount of durability and can't break any ores except for coal. The advantage of a gold pickaxe is that it mines the fastest.

Smelting with the furnace

After you have the basic components, you'll want to build a furnace to take your tool- and item-building skills to the next level. The furnace is a block to smelt ores and other items and blocks. It works similarly to the crafting table, and often people like to put a furnace near the crafting table as they craft new recipes.

To craft a furnace, on the crafting table, place cobblestone in the same formation as a chest, 8 pieces of cobblestone in a circle, with an empty slot in the middle. Crafting it gives you 1 furnace. Select the furnace in the inventory to place it on the ground (see Figure 1-12).

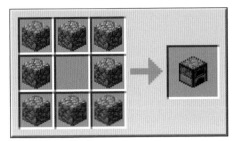

Figure 1-12: Building the furnace in the crafting grid.

After you place the furnace on the ground, right-click it to open the Smelting menu. There you can give the furnace fuel at the bottom and the item you want to smelt at the top (see Figure 1-13).

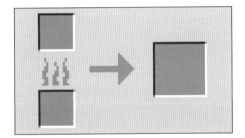

Figure 1-13: Smelting your first ore in the furnace.

When smelting, the furnace changes textures and gives off light. The texture of the furnace almost looks like a polished cobblestone with two holes in the front. When smelting, the two holes turn orange and red, as in a fire. When the smelting ends, the texture returns to normal, and you see the new ore or item next to the furnace.

Digging dirt with a shovel

The shovel, like the pickaxe, is a tool to dig certain blocks faster, such as grass, dirt, sand, and even mycelium.

To craft a shovel, in the crafting table, place 2 sticks in the middle in a vertical arrangement, and place 1 block according to the tier (as shown in Figure 1-14). Crafting gives you 1 shovel. Table 1-2 tells you all about the different types of shovels.

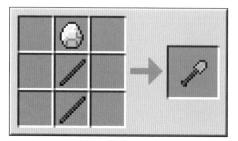

Figure 1-14: Crafting a shovel lets you dig certain blocks in Minecraft.

Table 1-2		Crafting Shovels	
Shovel	**Type**	**Craft with This Item**	**Use It to Dig . . .**
	Wood	Wooden plank	Snow, Dirt, Sand, and Soul Sand
	Stone	Cobblestone	Snow, Dirt, Sand, and Soul Sand
	Iron	Iron ingot	Anything
	Gold	Gold ingot	Anything
	Diamond	Diamond	Anything

Chopping trees with the ax

The *ax* is a tool that lets you chop down wooden blocks faster.

The appearance of the ax within the crafting table looks like a stick with an ax head on it. To craft the ax, place 2 sticks in the middle of the crafting table grid in a vertical arrangement, and place 3 blocks according to the tier — two on top and one just below the one on top (see Figure 1-15 for an example). This recipe gives you 1 ax. Table 1-3 explains what the tiers of axes can chop.

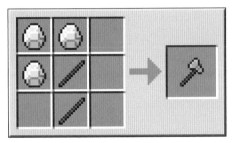

Figure 1-15: Crafting the ax lets you chop down trees and other wooden blocks faster.

Table 1-3   Crafting Axes

Ax	Type	Craft with This Item	Use It to Chop This
	Wood	Wooden plank	Vines, mushrooms, Cocoa, Daylight sensors
	Stone	Cobblestone	Vines, mushrooms, Cocoa, Daylight sensors (and anything wood chops well)
	Iron	Iron ingot	Jack O' Lanterns, Signs, Pumpkins, Note blocks, pressure plates (and any lower tiers)
	Gold	Gold ingot	Anything
	Diamond	Diamond	Bookshelves (and any lower tiers)

Tilling ground with a hoe

The *hoe* is used to turn dirt and grass blocks into farmland for producing wheat, melons, pumpkins, carrots, or potatoes. To till, right-click on a grass or dirt block while holding a hoe.

The material used in the construction of the hoe has almost no effect on the utility of the hoe — the process of tilling is effectively instantaneous, regardless of material, and all hoes deal the same damage as fists if used in combat. As with all tools, the material used does, however, affect the durability of the hoe.

Breaking normal blocks, such as dirt, with a hoe doesn't affect its durability, and the hoe takes as long to break the block as your fist would. Because all hoes take the same length of time to till dirt, constructing golden hoes (low durability) or diamond hoes (waste of diamonds) is usually impractical.

To craft a hoe, place 2 sticks in the middle in a vertical arrangement on the crafting table, and place two blocks at the top according to the tier (see Figure 1-16). This recipe gives you 1 hoe.

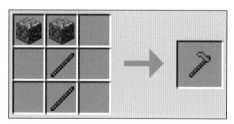

Figure 1-16: Crafting a cobblestone hoe to till ground and turn dirt for farmland.

2
Defending Yourself

In This Chapter

▸ Crafting weapons

▸ Protecting yourself by crafting armor

Surviving the elements, mobs, and other players is a vital part of mastering Minecraft. Crafting a sword is a necessary step early in the game (often accomplished on the first day). As the game progresses, you'll appreciate the advantages of investing in higher quality weapons so that you can attack effectively. Also, try to craft high-quality (and sometimes even fashionable) armor to protect yourself. This chapter gives you recipes that help you defend yourself.

Creating a Sword

The sword does more damage than any other weapon and is therefore the most valuable weapon. Your sword can help you fight mobs and break blocks quickly.

Like the pickaxe, the sword has five tiers of strength. Here they are, in order from least to greatest:

1. Wood
2. Gold
3. Stone
4. Iron
5. Diamond

When you use a sword to break blocks or fight, you decrease its durability. Both tools and weapons have durability bars, which are displayed on the bottom of the item in the inventory slot. When the durability bar becomes small and red, swords need to be repaired using the correct ingredients on a crafting grid or an anvil. (For the anvil recipe, see Chapter 5.) However, a sword doesn't need to be repaired as often as a pickaxe or shovel does. Also, the diamond sword has such high durability that it almost always lasts throughout the game without needing repair.

As the preceding list indicates, gold is less durable than stone or iron. Because gold is usually scarce and is needed in other recipes (primarily, in brewing and potions), making a gold sword usually isn't the best use of gold. The exception occurs when you enchant your sword, because gold is the best medium for enchanting. An enchanted sword can have special capabilities, depending on the enchantment you use, as you discover in Chapter 8.

The texture of a sword includes a pummel, handle, guard, and blade. The various tiers affect the textures.

To craft a sword, place one stick and two blocks in your crafting grid as shown in Figure 2-1. The blocks you use depend on the tier — two wooden planks, two cobblestone, or two iron ingots, for example.

Wood sword

Gold sword

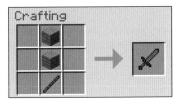

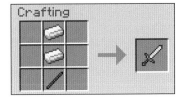

Stone sword

Iron sword

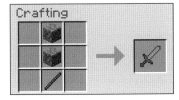

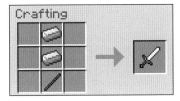

Diamond sword

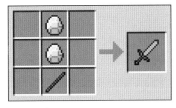

Figure 2-1: Creating a sword.

Stringing Your Bow

The bow inflicts different amounts of damage, depending on how much it's charged.

The relationship between your bow and arrow, and the defense your arrow provides has a few layers:

- ✔ The more charge the bow has, the farther the arrow travels.

- ✔ The farther the arrow travels, the stronger the arrow becomes.

- ✔ The stronger the arrow, the slower your player moves as you charge back the bow.

⤙ The slower your player moves, the more zoomed-in the camera gets, allowing you to better aim at your target.

⤙ The slower you move and the more zoomed-in the camera gets, the better the accuracy of your shot.

A fully charged bow inflicts 4½ hearts of damage, with the rare chance of inflicting 5. (We can't tell at what point the target gets 5 hearts and at what point they get 4½ hearts — it seems random to us.) When the bow isn't charged, it deals only half a heart.

The bow has four different textures: one default and three charging. The default texture has a shaft and a hand grip along with a string. The three other textures show a stretched string along with an arrow, ready to be fired. Each texture increasingly stretches the bow string. When your bow string is fully stretched, your bow is fully charged to shoot at full potential!

To craft the bow, follow these steps on your crafting grid (see Figure 2-2):

1. **Place a stick at the bottom middle position.**

2. **Place a stick in the middle position to the right or left.**

3. **Put a stick in the middle top position.**

4. **Place three strings in a vertical column, as shown in Figure 2-2, where the stick at the end is not located. (If the stick is to the left, place the string to the right.)**

   You've created the bow!

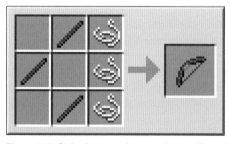

Figure 2-2: Stringing your bow on the crafting grid.

The bow, like many other crafted items, can be used as an ingredient in redstone. Chapter 4 covers redstone recipes.

You cannot use the bow without arrows.

Crafting an Arrow

When you fire an arrow from a bow, you can significantly damage a mob from a distance (whereas a sword must be used at close range). When the bow is at the perfect angle and is fully charged, you can shoot the arrow a total of 120 blocks away — that's a lot of blocks! The arrow travels in an arc, and you can retrieve the arrows you have fired. Arrows shot by skeletons (a type of mob in Minecraft) cannot be retrieved, and neither can arrows fired from an infinity bow (an enchanted bow that never runs out of arrows that you or other players can shoot).

The texture of an arrow consists of the arrow head at the top, the stick in the middle, and the feathers *(fletching)* at the end.

You can craft four arrows at a time by placing a flint, a stick, and a feather in the crafting grid, as shown in Figure 2-3.

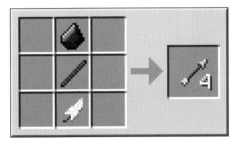

Figure 2-3: Crafting an arrow.

Protecting Yourself with Armor

Armor protects you from hostile mobs (and other players) and from other items in the game, such as chicken eggs, falling anvils, lightning, cacti, and explosions. However, armor does not protect you in situations such as falling into the void, suffocating, or drowning (except in certain situations where the armor is enchanted, such as the respiration enchantment that enchants your helmet to allow you to stay underwater longer).

On the inventory display screen, the armor slots appear in the upper left corner. As you can see in Figure 2-4, you have a slot for each of these items:

- Helmet
- Chestplate
- Leggings
- Boots

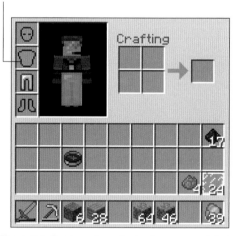

Figure 2-4: The inventory display has armor slots in the upper left corner.

Like the quality rating for swords, armor comes in tiers, from least effective to most effective:

1. Leather
2. Golden
3. Chain
4. Iron
5. Diamond

You cannot craft chain armor but can obtain it from mob drops or by trading with villagers. When it loses durability, you can repair it on a crafting table with iron ingots or on an anvil. You can also enchant chain armor.

Leather

Leather is the least durable, but most common beginning armor material. It is normally acquired by killing cows, but it can also be crafted from rabbit hide. To craft, place 4 rabbit hides into a square shape in the crafting grid yielding one piece of leather (see Figure 2-5).

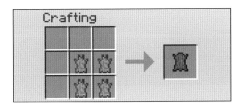

Figure 2-5: The rabbit leather recipe looks like this.

Though leather and golden armor are the least desirable materials for protection, they are the easiest to enchant. Also, leather armor can be dyed, as we explain Chapter 7. Figure 2-6 shows leather armor, with a yellow-dyed cap, a red-dyed tunic, a green-dyed pants, and blue-dyed boots.

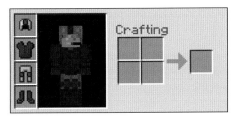

Figure 2-6: Dyeing leather armor.

Like the pickaxe and sword, armor loses durability over time. (See the durability bar to learn how much durability you have left.) You repair armor in a crafting grid or on an anvil (see Chapter 5 to learn how to do this).

When you repair enchanted armor on the crafting grid, your repaired item has slightly more durability but loses any enchantments. However, if you repair the armor on an anvil, the armor remains enchanted.

Not all pieces of armor need to be made of the same material. For example, a player can wear a leather helmet with a diamond chestplate and iron leggings. As rare ingredients become available, such as diamond, improving a single piece of armor is extremely beneficial.

Armor provides defense points, shown as half a shirt of armor on the Armor bar above the Health bar (see Figure 2-7). The higher the number of defense points, the lower amount of damage is dealt to the player in an attack. Many players craft or obtain a full set of armor early in the game to maximize their defense points.

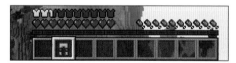

Figure 2-7: Defense points are shown above the Health bar as half a shirt of armor.

Donning your helmet

A *helmet* (or *cap,* when it's made of leather) protects your avatar's head in an attack. The helmet provides better protection than boots because the helmet provides more defense points generally. A leather helmet provides only 1 defense point (represented by half a shirt), and a diamond helmet provides 3.

When enchanted with the respiration enchantment, a helmet can extend your underwater breathing time. When enchanted with the aqua affinity enchantment, a helmet can increase the underwater mining rate.

To craft a helmet, place 5 matching items (leather or iron ingots, for example) into a crafting grid in a helmet formation. That is, place 3 pieces on top and 1 piece below on either side (see Figure 2-8).

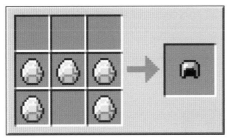

Figure 2-8: Crafting a helmet on the crafting grid.

Pounding your chestplate

The *chestplate* (or *tunic,* when it's in leather form) is stored in the second inventory slot and provides protection for the upper body.

A chestplate provides significantly more protection than a helmet due to the increased defense points the chestplate gives you. So, craft your chestplate first if you have sufficient ingredients and upgrade to a stronger material as soon as possible.

To craft, you place 8 identical items (leather or gold ingots, for example) into a crafting grid, as shown in Figure 2-9. Notice how the recipe is shaped roughly like a shirt in the crafting grid.

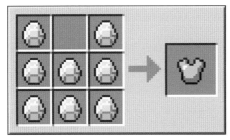

Figure 2-9: To create a chestplate, place items on the crafting grid as shown here.

Putting on leggings

Leggings (or *pants*), which are stored in the third inventory slot, provide the second-highest level of protection.

You should craft this piece of armor early in the game and upgrade it whenever materials become available.

The recipe for leggings requires 7 identical items to be placed in an arch shape that looks like pants (see Figure 2-10).

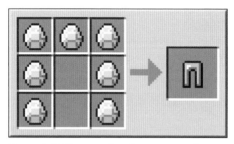

Figure 2-10: To put on leggings, arrange items on the crafting grid as shown here.

Walking in boots

The least effective piece of armor, and the one stored at the bottom of the inventory screen, is boots. But don't be fooled into thinking that boots are not a vital part of armor. They offer defense points, and they can be enchanted for additional properties. Boots that are enchanted with a depth strider enchantment increase underwater speed; boots enchanted with a feather falling enchantment reduce fall damage. See Chapter 8 for more boot enchantments.

To craft a pair of boots, you need only four items, arranged as shown in Figure 2-11.

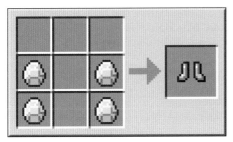

Figure 2-11: To wear boots, arrange your items this way.

 Though all items can be enchanted with various abilities, helmets and boots have unique enchantments that make them particularly important pieces of armor despite the low number of defense points they provide.

Armor Stand

The magnificent armor stand is a true marvel. The closest things that we had for display were chests and other mobs. In Survival mode you can only currently place armor and mob heads on to armor stands. In Creative mode, customizing the NBT tag will allow you to add arms; rotate the head arms and legs; take away the bottom plate; make the armor stand invisible; make it not have gravity; and even make a mini one!

Just right-click the armor stand to put on and take off armor. Another cool feature about the armor stand is that it is an entity. That means it has gravity, can be picked up with minecarts, and can even be moved with pistons.

At the bottom of an armor stand is a stone slab plate. The legs are two sticks, which extend all the way to the shoulders. The waist is one horizontal stick, along with the shoulders. The head is one vertical stick.

To craft, place a stone slab at the bottom middle, then place two sticks above that slab. Finally place sticks in the four corners of the crafting table (see Figure 2-12).

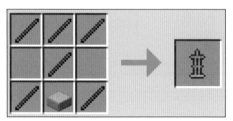

Figure 2-12: Creating an armor stand.

3
Advancing By Way of Farming and Mining

In This Chapter

- Harvesting food and food items
- Smelting food
- Creating utensils
- Mining and smelting ore
- Crafting mineral blocks

*A*fter you have created the essential items on the first night to survive a mob attack, you must begin harvesting food and ore. The Hunger bar will quickly deplete, which also drains the Health bar when you don't have a supply of food. For this reason, you need to craft and farm food items to keep yourself well-nourished throughout the game. This chapter provides the recipes that are necessary to craft food items and the utensils to create prosperous farms and well-fed players.

For the parents out there, crafting and farming food items are some of Jesse's favorite activities, because it teaches kids who play Minecraft some basic cooking skills — and a little nutrition in the process.

Harvesting and Farming Food Items

Ironically, many of the items that we think of as food, such as pumpkins and sugar, are not eaten in Minecraft, though they are used in other ways. Some items produce seeds as well, and both the seeds and the items that those seeds produce can be used throughout the game. This section covers food items that supply food points when you eat them and food-like items that are commonly farmed for other reasons.

Bonemeal is used as fertilizer when growing crops. Bonemeal speeds the growth of carrots, seeds, cocoa beans, and potatoes. It can instantly grow saplings and mushrooms, but a lot of bonemeal and a little luck (not to mention enough space to grow) are required. Many players load a dispenser with bonemeal to automate fertilizing. Wheat farming in particular requires bonemeal to grow at an efficient rate. However, bonemeal doesn't help nether wart, cacti, sugar cane, or vines to grow. Bonemeal is also used in dyes, and you find the recipe for bonemeal in Chapter 7.

Crafting seeds from melons

A melon farm is one of the more difficult farms to start, because seeds are difficult to find. They can be made from melon blocks, found in the jungle biome, or collected from slices acquired by trading with villagers. Rarely, you find melon blocks in a dungeon chest.

After you have acquired melon slices, likely from a villager, you can craft melon seeds. To craft melon seeds, simply place a slice anywhere on the grid (see Figure 3-1). The resulting seeds can be planted.

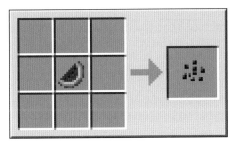

Figure 3-1: Crafting melon seeds from a melon.

However, like all plants, melon seeds need light in order to grow. Unlike certain plants, melons need an adjacent dirt, grass, or farmland block. If an opaque block is above a melon plant's stem, the plant won't grow. After the melon plant fully matures, it produces a melon block. One melon plant can produce again and again.

Crafting blocks to store melons

If you have the need to store multiple melons, a block is an effective way to store the melons. A block takes only 1 inventory slot, but contains multiple melons to feed you on your journey.

A melon block can be crafted from 9 melon slices, fully filling the crafting grid (see Figure 3-2). This process cannot be reversed, so to change a block into slices, it has to be placed and broken. The result is usually 3 to 7 slices.

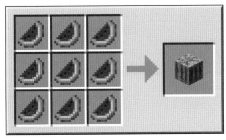

Figure 3-2: Crafting a melon block from 9 melon slices.

Because breaking a melon block is a significant loss in number of slices, melon blocks are rarely crafted (though they're frequently harvested on a farm). The only reason to craft blocks is to stack them into a single inventory slot, allowing a significant supply of food for a journey.

When a melon block is broken, it yields only 3 to 7 of the 9 melon slices that were used to craft it.

Farming pumpkin seeds

Pumpkins can be quite useful as you make your way through Minecraft. Pumpkins are a necessary ingredient in making the following:

- A snow golem and an iron golem, which can be used as a mask-like helmet
- Jack-o-lanterns
- Pumpkin pie

Pumpkins are not actually food. Pumpkin seeds are crafted by placing a pumpkin anywhere on the grid (see Figure 3-3). Pumpkins are commonly found in most overland biomes, and their seeds can be found in chests, usually in abandoned mineshafts within the Extreme Hills biome.

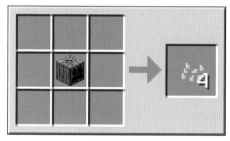

Figure 3-3: Crafting pumpkin seeds from a pumpkin.

To farm, pumpkin seeds require a soil block similar to melons. Another common use for pumpkin seeds is to breed chickens (to do so, hold seeds and right-click on 2 chickens).

Feeding your sugar tooth

Sugar is not actually a food source and cannot be eaten alone. Though it's an ingredient in cake and pumpkin pie (which supplies hunger points), sugar is more commonly used in brewing and in working with horses, because sugar can help tame, heal, and increase the growth rate of horses.

To craft, place one sugar cane on the crafting grid (see Figure 3-4).

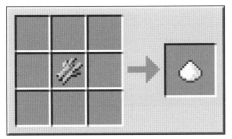

Figure 3-4: Crafting sugar with sugar cane on the crafting grid.

Making bread, cake, and cookies

Everyone loves yummy baked goods! Like flour in real life, bread, cake, and cookies all require wheat as a main ingredient. Many players begin a wheat farm on their first or second day.

Seeds are abundant in most biomes, and seeds can be obtained by breaking weeds you find throughout the biome. However, you need a light source — simply the sun supplemented with torches. Also as in real life, wheat grows best when given bone-meal to act as a fertilizer.

As on most farms, growing wheat can be time-consuming, and can require automation using recipes from Chapter 4, like a hopper for automatically harvesting wheat into a chest. Wheat is also extremely useful in breeding cows and mooshrooms, as well as other animals in the game, which supply a significant amount of food.

Making bread

Bread is one of the easiest and most common food sources that is created early in the game because it requires only 3 wheat stalks, placed in a horizontal row, to craft (see Figure 3-5). No furnace or fuel is required to "bake" the bread. Increasingly, players are turning to mushrooms (turned into stew) and carrots as a food source rather than bread and using wheat in other ways.

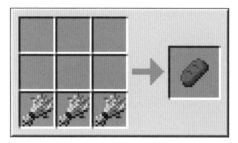

Figure 3-5: Crafting bread from wheat stalks on the crafting grid.

Baking a cake

Unlike other food items that are consumed when held, cake is a block that is eaten when placed. Each cake consists of six slices, which can be consumed by a single player or a group (as in a real-life celebration). If a single player eats only part of the cake, that player cannot pick up the remaining cake but can return to eat it later.

Because cake has multiple slices, it can restore up to 6 Hunger bars (1 bar per slice) but has a low saturation score (so you become hungry again quickly). Cake can also be used as mounting for a TNT cannon.

The biggest drawback to making cake is the complexity of the recipe. It requires 3 buckets of milk placed on the top row, a sugar-egg-sugar configuration for the second row, and 3 wheat stalks on the bottom row (see Figure 3-6). Before you can make a cake, you need to do the following:

- ✓ **Craft 3 milk buckets.** We explain how later in this chapter.

- ✓ **Craft sugar.** See the earlier section, "Feeding your sugar tooth."

- ✓ **Collect wheat and an egg.** You can find wheat by following the steps the upcoming section, "Making wheat and hay bales." You can find eggs anywhere you find chickens.

After you complete the recipe, the buckets return to the inventory.

Figure 3-6: Baking a cake on the crafting grid.

Baking cookies

Cookies require cocoa beans, which can be found in dungeon chests, which, in turn, are most commonly found in the jungle biomes, or on jungle trees. In a jungle biome, harvesting cocoa beans is easy, and crafting cookies is more advantageous than bread. The total hunger points for cookies is higher (per number of wheat stalks used), but because the saturation is lower, you need to eat more often. Many players consider cookies to be more of a rare treat and a novelty item than a long-term food source.

Cocoa beans can also be farmed, and mass-produced like other crops using jungle logs as the "soil."

To craft, place 2 stalks of wheat on either side of a cocoa bean in a horizontal row (see Figure 3-7). This recipe yields 8 cookies, which can be stacked.

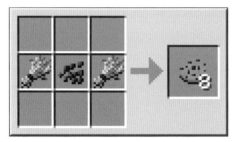

Figure 3-7: Baking cookies on the crafting grid.

Making pumpkin pie

Like many "junk foods," pumpkin pie provides a large number of hunger points (8) but has an extremely low saturation rate. This recipe quickly restores hunger points in times when your player needs to find a more saturation-dense food, such as meat. Unlike cake, pumpkin pie requires no milk buckets. Neither does it require a furnace or crafting table, so pumpkin pie is relatively easy to craft.

To make a pumpkin pie, simply place 1 pumpkin, 1 sugar, and 1 egg on a crafting grid (see Figure 3-8). This recipe is shapeless, so ingredients can go anywhere on the grid.

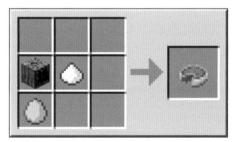

Figure 3-8: Creating the shapeless pumpkin pie recipe on the crafting grid.

Brewing mushroom stew

If you're in a mushroom-rich biome, harvesting mushrooms in addition to meat sources provides ample food. *Mushroom stew* (sometimes referred to as *soup*) is a shapeless recipe that is crafted by placing a bowl, a red mushroom, and a brown mushroom anywhere on a crafting grid (see Figure 3-9). The bowl will be returned to the player upon consumption.

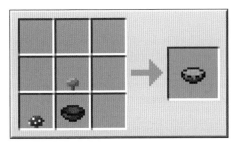

Figure 3-9: Making mushroom stew.

Mushrooms are occasionally farmed (an impractical and slow process) but also found abundantly in certain biomes, including the swamp, forest, and, of course, Mushroom Islands.

The stew cannot be stacked, so it must be consumed. However, the individual ingredients (bowls and mushrooms) can be stacked and stored so that food can be easily crafted as you continue through the game.

Mushrooms cannot be eaten alone unless they're crafted into stew. Mushrooms are also used in red dye (see Chapter 7) and in brewing fermented spider eyes (see Chapter 8).

Making wheat and hay bales

Wheat and hay bales are two more items that are not food in and of themselves. You craft them by placing 9 wheat stalks into the grid (see Figure 3-10), which allows for the compact storage of wheat that can be stacked in the inventory and used whenever you need to eat. You first break the hay bale back into wheat and then make bread (or other wheat-based recipes).

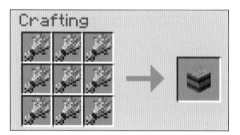

Figure 3-10: Making hay bales from wheat.

When you break a hay bale, the bale returns all 9 wheat stalks. To break the bale, place it anywhere on the crafting grid, essentially reversing the recipe. Doing a little math shows that 1 inventory slot with a full stack of 64 hay bales can be used to make 192 loaves of bread.

Many players stack hay bales in the inventory before beginning a long mining journey. Hay bales can also be used to feed horses, donkeys, or mules, which is why wheat farming is common. Hay bales can also heal animals and help foals grow into mature horses much faster. A common trick is to craft bread from the wheat and feed that bread to foals for maximum efficiency. Wheat not only helps breed animals by initiating Love mode but can also help tame a horse by decreasing the animal's temper.

Wheat and hay bales are an accepted food source that is used more effectively with animals. Animals not only yield better food sources than consuming wheat directly (through bread, cake, or cookies) but also provide other ingredients, such as leather for armor or books used in enchantments.

Though a vegetarian can find enough food sources to survive, the majority of Minecraft players eat almost exclusively from animal sources. (This is survival, after all!) Players also rely on animals for leather, which is essential to make books that are used in advanced enchanting (see Chapter 8).

Making the golden carrot

Carrot farms generally are fast outpacing any other type of farm on Minecraft. The yield is higher than wheat and offers players a similar number of hunger points.

The golden carrot is the highest-saturation food that's offered in the game. It is also the main ingredient in the potion of night vision (which leads to one of Thomas's favorite potions, the potion of invisibility). See Chapter 8 for more enchantment and brewing recipes such as the potion of night vision or potion of invisibility.

This recipe requires that 1 carrot be placed in the center square and surrounded by 8 gold nuggets (see Figure 3-11).

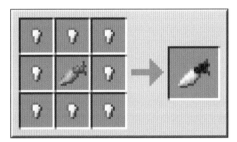

Figure 3-11: Creating the golden carrot with 1 carrot and 8 gold nuggets.

Crafting golden apples

Even better than a golden carrot, the rare golden apple not only restores hunger points but also provides 2 hearts on the Health bar. Consequently, the golden apple is the only food that can be eaten even when you have full hunger points. It's also used to cure a zombie villager.

To craft, place an apple in the center square, surrounded by 9 gold ingots (not nuggets — see Figure 3-12). A golden apple requires 9 times the amount of gold used in crafting a golden carrot.

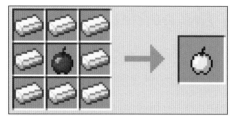

Figure 3-12: Creating a golden apple with an apple and 9 gold ingots.

Retrieving the enchanted golden apple

Enchanted golden apples are sometimes referred to by players as notch apples or god apples. (The name is a nod to the original maker of the game, Markus Persson, who goes by Notch.) The enchanted golden apple provides the regeneration of 90 health hearts and both resistance and fire resistance for 5 minutes. That's enough health restoration to survive any mob attack except for the void.

Another advantage is that golden apples are crafted, not brewed, so they can occur earlier in gameplay if a source of gold is found. Unfortunately, enchanted golden apples are extremely rare because they require an extreme amount of gold.

To craft, place an apple in the center square, surrounded by 9 *blocks* of gold (see Figure 3-13). That represents 72 gold ingots, or 648 gold nuggets.

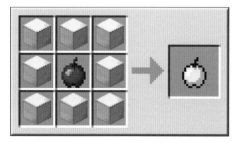

Figure 3-13: Crafting the enchanted golden apple, or notch apple.

Making beetroot soup

This incredibly nourishing soup heals 4 health hearts, but can be found only in the Pocket Edition. Beetroot is less common than wheat but provides three times the health when crafted into soup, compared to wheat-based bread.

To craft the soup, place the beetroots with a bowl, as shown in Figure 3-14. See the section "Building Utensils" later in this chapter for details about making a bowl.

Figure 3-14: Making beetroot soup on the crafting grid.

Cooking rabbit stew

Rabbit stew is a recipe that's new to Minecraft 1.8. Although the recipe is complicated, it provides an incredible 10 hunger points and 12 saturation points, ranking it as a cross between cake and a golden carrot. However, most players will find that eating the separate ingredients is more effective, because eating them separately still provides more hunger and saturation points.

To craft, place cooked rabbit in the top middle slot, add a carrot, and then baked potato, and then a mushroom (of either type) in the middle row, and place a bowl in the bottom middle slot (see Figure 3-15).

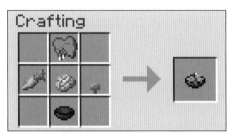

Figure 3-15: Making rabbit stew, with its various complicated ingredients.

Smelting Food

In addition to crafting food items, you can smelt (or cook) raw meat, fish, and potatoes. Doing so provides you with two to three times the amount of food points when compared to eating those items raw. Additionally, as in real life, raw chicken has a 30 percent chance of poisoning you, so you should cook all chicken (usually in a furnace) before eating it.

To cook food in a furnace (see Chapter 1 to learn how to make a furnace), simply place one piece of the raw food in the top of the furnace, and add a fuel source to the bottom of the furnace. (Your fuel source is likely to be coal, charcoal, or wood early in the game; see Figure 3-16 and Table 4-1.) This yields 1 cooked food item. Pork, beef, mutton (sheep), rabbit, chicken, fish, salmon, and potatoes can now be baked.

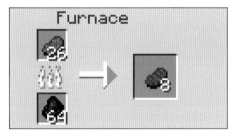

Figure 3-16: Smelting food in the furnace.

Table 4-1		Food Smelting Recipes		
Raw Food Icon	Item Name	Cooked Food Icon	Hunger Points	Saturation Level
	Pork chop		4	12.8
	Steak		4	12.8
	Mutton		6	9.6
	Rabbit		5	6
	Chicken		6	7.2
	Fish		5	6
	Salmon		6	9.6
	Potato		6	7.2

Building Utensils

After you understand food recipes and other food-related items, you need to craft the objects that are used when you're working with animals and food sources.

Building a fishing rod

Fishing rods are far more useful than most players realize. Obviously, their primary use is to catch fish, which are abundant and a good source of food. But fishing rods can also reel in junk or treasure (just as in real life).

An unenchanted rod has an 85 percent chance of catching fish, a 10 percent chance of catching junk, and a 5 percent chance of hauling in some treasure. The odds of catching treasure increase with enchantment. Treasures include a bow, an enchanted book, an enchanted fishing rod, a saddle, name tags, and lily pads.

Ironically, the junk may not be worthless. If you reel in sticks, string, leather, or tripwire hook, you can use all these items in recipes throughout this book. You can also use fishing rods to hook mobs, boats, and minecarts or to activate pressure plates.

Like other tools, such as swords or pickaxes, a fishing rod has limited durability and can be used only 65 times before breaking.

To craft a fishing rod, place 3 sticks in an upward diagonal with 2 strings in the lower right blocks (see Figure 3-17).

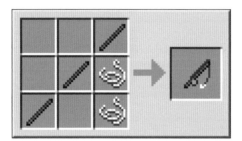

Figure 3-17: Building a fishing rod with 3 sticks and 2 strings.

Fishing while raining increases the chance of making a good catch.

Creating a bucket

A bucket is a useful tool for carrying milk, water, and lava. Milk buckets are used in the cake recipe (as described earlier in this chapter), and you can drink the milk in a bucket to offset all effects — most notably, poison. Buckets are also used to carry water, which can then be dropped as a block back into the environment. This feature becomes quite handy in farming.

Water buckets are also used to fill cauldrons for potions and to put out fires. Lava buckets let you transport and drop the lava back into the environment, which can be used to create a barrier against a mob, to produce obsidian or cobblestone, to create weapons, and as a long-lasting fuel source for a furnace.

A bucket is crafted by placing 3 iron ingots in a V pattern in the grid, roughly forming the shape of a bucket (see Figure 3-18).

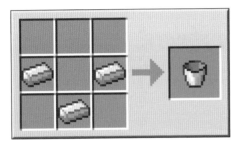

Figure 3-18: Creating a bucket on the crafting grid.

Building bowls

Bowls have limited usefulness because they're used only to hold mushroom stew and beetroot soup. (They can also be used to "milk" a mooshroom, which produces stew, not milk.) Bowls cannot be used in place of buckets to hold milk, lava, or water.

A mooshroom is a cow found in the mushroom biome. It is red, with white spots, and has brown and red mushrooms growing on it.

To craft 4 bowls, place 3 wood planks in a V shape (see Figure 3-19).

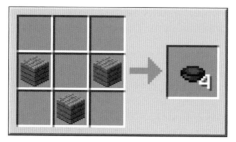

Figure 3-19: Making a bowl on the crafting grid with 3 wood planks.

Both mushrooms and bowls are stackable so, in a mushroom-rich biome, harvesting and stacking them in your inventory can provide an excellent portable food source.

Crafting shears

Shears can significantly increase wool production by allowing you to shear a sheep for up to 3 blocks and leaving the sheep alive to regrow more wool. Without shears, you can harvest wool only by killing a sheep, yielding 1 block of wool.

Many players create sheep farms, occasionally dyeing the sheep and, consequently, the wool for use in redstone or other recipes. Shears can also be used to harvest leaves, grass, ferns, bushes, and vines. Shears are used to collect string from cobwebs and to cut a tripwire without creating a redstone pulse.

Technically, shears can clip the red mushroom off a mooshroom, which would change it back into a normal cow. However, mooshrooms are rare and valuable, so you would be unlikely to do that. Like most tools, shears lose durability over time and can be enchanted on an anvil.

To craft shears, place 2 iron ingots in an upward diagonal (see Figure 3-20).

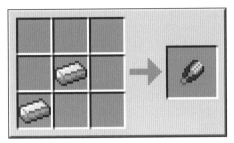

Figure 3-20: Crafting sheers from 2 iron ingots.

Building fences

The primary use of a fence is to keep animals in and to keep mobs out. Fences technically take up only 1 block space but function as 1½ spaces tall, preventing players and mobs (but not spiders) from jumping over them. Proper lighting inside a fenced area also limits mob attacks. Meanwhile, fences keep animals contained so that players can farm them effectively.

Fences are also used as guardrails along bridges and even balconies, and you can fish over them. Another immense advantage is that players can see through fences like glass, though mobs cannot see in.

Fences are particularly useful in underwater construction. They're not a full solid block, so they can be used to create air pockets without the water dripping in, which is useful in creating a water elevator, fence walls, or a waterproof door.

Often used to create bridges (when combined with pressure plates) or shallow stairs (for sprinting), fences also allow passive mobs to be tethered to the fence by using a lead (as described later in this chapter, in the section "Taking the lead"). The main disadvantage is when a block is placed close to the fence — a mob can then use that block to jump the fence. Endermen are particularly notorious for this trick.

To craft a fence, simply place 2 sticks in a vertical column in the middle with 4 wooden planks on either side. This recipe yields 3 fence pieces (see Figure 3-21).

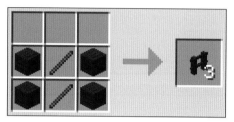

Figure 3-21: Building fence pieces with 6 sticks.

Making a fence gate

A fence gate functions as a door and always opens away from you. It must be placed on a block, but remains if the block is later mined away. A major advantage is that the fence gate prevents the flow of water and lava even when open (though the gate may catch fire).

Unlike with a door, zombies cannot break through a fence gate, and villagers cannot open one. Fence gates can also be manipulated through redstone such as pressure plates.

To craft a fence gate, place a stick, and then a wood plank, and then another stick on two horizontal rows (see Figure 3-22).

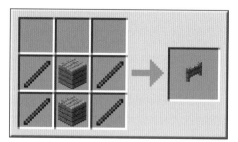

Figure 3-22: The fence gate recipe looks like this.

Building cobblestone walls

Cobblestone walls function like fences and are considered a decorative alternative to their wooden counterparts. Like fences, they keep out most mobs, but beware: Neither fences nor cobblestone walls can block skeleton arrows, and spiders can still crawl over cobblestone walls.

A cobblestone wall does have a higher blast tolerance than a fence when a creeper explodes, but a cobblestone wall isn't blast-proof. Cobblestone walls come in two forms: basic and mossy.

To craft, place 6 cobblestones (or moss stones) in two horizontal rows (see Figure 3-23 and 3-24). Each recipe yields 6 wall pieces. The recipe for moss stone, along with several other decorative blocks, is in Chapter 6. A moss stone wall is just a decorative type of wall.

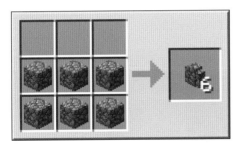

Figure 3-23: The cobblestone wall recipe looks like this.

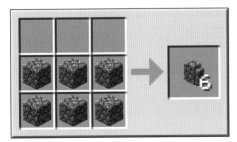

Figure 3-24: The moss stone wall recipe looks like this.

Building a nether brick fence

Nether brick fences are similar to wooden fences, but they're blast-resistant and fireproof, making them particularly effective against the ghast, one of the most dangerous creatures in the Nether. Nether brick fences also shield light sources, which can be used to affect spawning mobs and growing plants.

A nether brick fence connects to fence gates, allowing you to build a maze by using a mixture of nether brick and wooden fence gate pieces. The nether brick fence confuses most mobs, with the exception of zombies because they can't see it. The nether brick fence will likely slow down zombies rather than stop them altogether. Though nether brick fences connect to gates and most blocks, they do not connect to wooden fences.

To craft nether brick fence pieces, place 6 nether bricks (found in fortresses in the Nether, or crafted using the recipe in Chapter 6) into two horizontal rows, yielding 6 fence pieces (see Figure 3-25).

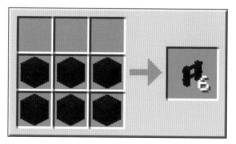

Figure 3-25: Building a nether brick fence.

The wooden fence recipe yields 3 pieces, and the stone and nether brick fence yield 6.

Taking the lead

Sometimes referred to as a leash, a *lead* is useful in several situations. Here are a few things you can do with a lead:

- **Lead a passive mob or tether it to a fence or a nether brick fence.** You can hold multiple leads at a time, but you need one lead per mob. The types of mobs and animals you can leash include horses, cats, wolves, squids, sheep, pigs, cows, mooshrooms, chickens, iron golems, and snow golems. The major exception is bats, which cannot be leashed.

  A mob can be tethered to a fence or player. When tethered to a player, the lead breaks if the mob passes through the nether portal. Also, the knot holding a lead to a fence can be broken with a bow and arrow (including arrows shot by skeletons).

- **Suspend mobs in the air.** However, in case the lead fails because the knot is broken from an arrow, the mob will likely sustain a fatal amount of fall damage.

- **Help tame ocelots.** When an ocelot is placed on a lead (the first step in taming an ocelot), it cannot run away from the player.

- **Lead a horse across deep water.**

To craft leads, place one slimeball in the center with 4 string pieces arranged as shown in Figure 3-26. This recipe yields 2 leads.

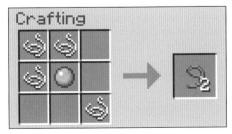

Figure 3-26: Making a lead on the crafting grid.

Mining Ore

Ores are the essential ingredient in tools and armor. Redstone ore, which is unique, allows players to create all sorts of devices and contraptions (see more in Chapter 5). Blocks are created from a significant amount of ore, allowing them to be stacked efficiently in the inventory. Many players mine and farm simultaneously. The rest of the chapter explores the various recipes related to mining.

Smelting Ore into Ingot

Smelting is similar to crafting but requires a furnace rather than a crafting table. See Chapter 1 to learn how to craft a furnace.

To smelt ore in your furnace, you must have a fuel source. Early in the game, here are the most common fuel sources: wooden planks, previously crafted wooden tools, or weapons that have been replaced with stone items. The other major source of fuel is coal, which is easily mined, or charcoal (see "Crafting coal blocks," later in this chapter).

Smelting an iron ingot

Iron ore is one of the most often used ingredients in crafting quality weapons, tools, buckets, flint, steel, and shears. It's easily mined but must be smelted into an ingot before it can be crafted.

To smelt, place iron ore in the top of the furnace and a fuel source in the bottom, to yield an iron ingot (see Figure 3-27).

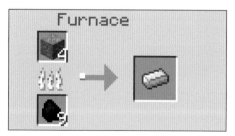

Figure 3-27: Smelting iron in the furnace produces an iron ingot.

Making gold ingots

Gold ore can be mined with an iron or diamond pickaxe (just hold the pickaxe and then hold down the mouse button to start mining). Gold ore is then smelted like iron into ingots. Gold ingots can further be crafted into nuggets. Ingots are necessary to make golden apples, powered rails, and clocks. To smelt, place gold ore in the top of the furnace and fuel in bottom to yield one gold ingot (see Figure 3-28).

Figure 3-28: A completed smelting of the gold ingot.

Burning charcoal

Charcoal is similar to coal but is smelted from wood, making it easy to create on your first night playing the game. This allows you to create a torch. Though slightly time-consuming, smelting charcoal from any wooden items yields a more efficient fuel than burning wood directly. To smelt, place any wood in the top of the furnace and any fuel in the bottom (commonly, another wood source; see Figure 3-29).

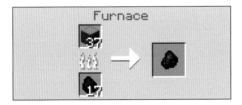

Figure 3-29: Smelting charcoal.

Crafting Blocks of Minerals

Minerals such as coal, emeralds, iron, and diamonds can be crafted into blocks and then crafted in reverse back into their individual components. Items can then be stacked in an inventory or provide other advantages, as discussed in the following sections.

Crafting coal blocks

When 9 pieces of coal are crafted into a block (see Figure 3-30), the resulting block can smelt 80 items, as compared to the 72 items that the individual coal pieces could smelt. However, you rarely need that much fuel at any given time, so coal blocks are largely crafted for inventory storage. Note that charcoal cannot be crafted into coal block or stacked with either coal or coal blocks.

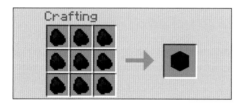

Figure 3-30: Making coal blocks from coal on the crafting grid.

Making diamond blocks and emerald blocks

You craft a block of diamond by placing 9 diamonds placed in the crafting grid, as shown in Figure 3-31. A diamond block is unusual, because diamonds themselves are rare, and the only function of the diamond block is to store or decorate.

Similarly, emerald blocks function only as storage or decoration. Though emeralds are fairly rare, found mostly in the hill biome or by way of village trading (and of course, found in unlimited numbers in Creative mode), their texture is unique and commonly used as a decorative block, particularly by advanced players. To create an emerald block, simply follow the diamond block recipe with emeralds instead of diamonds (see Figure 3-32).

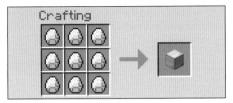

Figure 3-31: Producing diamond blocks from diamonds.

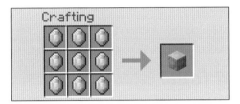

Figure 3-32: Making emerald blocks.

Producing gold blocks and nuggets

Nine gold ingots (made from smelting gold ore for each gold ingot) can be crafted into a block (see Figure 3-33) and the block can be reverse-crafted back into ingots. Gold blocks are necessary ingredients in enchanted golden apples and in building the nether portal in the PE edition (the version of Minecraft for mobile devices).

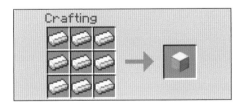

Figure 3-33: Crafting gold blocks from gold ingots.

Gold nuggets are crafted by placing one gold ingot in the crafting grid, yielding 9 nuggets (see Figure 3-34; this recipe can also be reversed). Because a nugget represents only one-ninth of an ingot, it's a significantly cheaper ingredient than in recipes that call for either ingots or blocks. Nuggets are used in firework stars (see Chapter 4), glistering melon (see Chapter 8), and the golden carrot (see earlier in this chapter, under "Making the Golden Carrot").

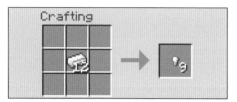

Figure 3-34: Making gold nuggets from gold ingots.

Crafting lapis lazuli blocks

The blue block of lapis lazuli, which functions like stone rather than ore, is used as a decorative block and an occasional trap because it looks like water (luring other players into jumping onto it). Like the other mineral blocks, a lapis lazuli block is crafted from 9 lapis lazuli stones (see Figure 3-35), and the block can be crafted back into the 9 stones.

Lapis lazuli is a common ingredient in dyes that are used to dye armor, wolf collars, firework stars, hardened clay, stained glass, and wool. The color and texture of lapis lazuli has also become one of Thomas's favorite colors in the game (among other players), and it's commonly used as a decorative block.

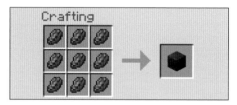

Figure 3-35: Crafting lapis lazuli.

Making redstone blocks

Redstone is one of the most powerful features in Minecraft. A redstone block, crafted from 9 redstones (see Figure 3-36), acts as a power source. When placed, a redstone block powers adjacent redstone dust, redstone repeaters, and redstone comparators. A redstone block also activates redstone components. It doesn't power adjacent opaque blocks.

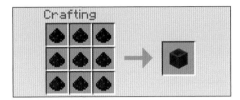

Figure 3-36: Making redstone blocks from redstone.

Producing iron blocks

Iron blocks are crafted from 9 iron ingots (see Figure 3-37). Remember that iron ingots are smelted from iron ore, as we explain in the earlier section, "Smelting an iron ingot."

Iron blocks are critical ingredients in iron golems and anvils.

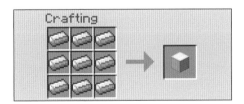

Figure 3-37: Making iron blocks.

Nether Quartz

Nether Quartz, as the name implies, can only be obtained in the Nether. It is a key ingredient in Daylight Sensors and Redstone Comparator as well as other quartz-based recipes (see Chapter 6). Nether Quartz is ready to use as soon as you mine it and does not need to be smelted.

Gold and iron ore must be smelted before being used as ingots. Coal, diamonds, emeralds, lapis lazuli, redstone, and Nether Quartz can be used immediately or crafted into blocks.

4
Advancing through Engineering

In This Chapter

▶ Finding and handling fire

▶ Getting around with different types transportation

▶ Engineering all sorts of items with redstone

*I*f you jumped directly to this chapter, you're not alone. Many players are eager to start blowing things up, developing sophisticated rails, and advancing their redstone capabilities. For the budding engineer who is eager to build rather than survive, farm, and mine, this chapter is written for you.

Discovering Fire

Fire, as in real life, is both helpful and dangerous. It provides light, cooks meat, ignites TNT, and causes damage to mobs. But it can also cause damage to players, burn their belongings and farms, and damage passive mobs. Learning to use fire correctly is vital as you advance through the game.

Crafting and lighting TNT

TNT is the only explosive block in the game. Lighting it on fire, by using flint and steel (see "Creating Fire with Flint and Steel" later in the chapter) sets it off. It toggles between a white texture and the normal texture; after the white texture appears eight times, the TNT expands quickly and explodes.

The explosion appears random but is determined by a complicated mathematical formula that's buried in the game's code.

Encasing TNT in stone blows up an exact 3-x-3 area. TNT, which is often used to blow up large amounts of space, can be lit by other explosions and blows up a couple of seconds afterward. TNT, once lit or activated, becomes an entity and can pass through other entities, though not solid blocks. It also responds to physics and will fall.

A massive TNT explosion from multiple TNT blocks has the ability to crash a server (so be respectful when you're using other people's servers).

Players can shield themselves from an explosion by hiding behind obsidian, bedrock, liquids (water or lava, for example), anvils, enchantment tables, ender chests, command blocks, and the end portal frame. Also, hiding in a minecart protects a player (or mob) from most of the damage.

TNT is a critical ingredient in a TNT cannon or arrow cannon, or to rocket-jump (when a player is a human cannonball requiring enchanted armor to survive). In addition to the sheer fun of blowing things up, TNT is an effective mining tool to blast away large areas. TNT is also interactive with redstone and can be used to create traps, including land mines.

The texture of TNT looks like a bunch of dynamite tied together by a white ribbon with the word *TNT* in the middle. At the top is a bunch of wicks. To craft TNT, you need 4 sand (either red or regular) and 5 gunpowder. Place the gunpowder in the four corners and in the middle, and then place the sand in the remaining squares to create a checkered pattern (see Figure 4-1).

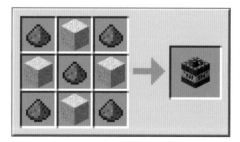

Figure 4-1: Creating TNT with sand and gunpowder.

Creating fire with flint and steel

As with Survival mode in real life, the combination of *flint and steel* is a way to create fire in Minecraft. You can use flint and steel to break blocks by left-clicking or to place fire by right-clicking. It also ignites TNT by right-clicking and can even detonate creepers.

To place fire correctly, you must right-click on top of a solid, fully opaque block or on the sides of a flammable block. Though flint and steel has unlimited durability when breaking blocks, it lasts through 65 right-click fire placements, even if the fire placement is done incorrectly.

Fire placement with flint and steel is often used in the following ways:

- ✔ Clear a forest.
- ✔ Take down a wooden structure such as a roof.
- ✔ Cook animals for food without a furnace.
- ✔ Create a barrier between a player and a mob.
- ✔ Light netherrack in the Nether.

Flint and steel is often craftable midgame, when a player has mined iron. After that point, its ingredients are usually fairly abundant. It can also be enchanted. The texture is iron in the shape of the letter *C* on top and a deformed flint texture at the bottom.

Flint and steel is a shapeless crafting recipe. To craft flint and steel, put an iron ingot and a piece of flint in the crafting grid (see Figure 4-2).

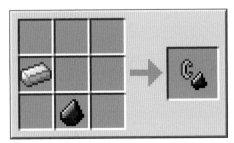

Figure 4-2: Crafting flint and steel with iron ingot and a piece of flint.

Building a fire charge

A *fire charge* functions like a single use flint and steel because the fire charge is consumed when used (like a used match). The fire charge can be shot from a dispenser, causing 5 points (2 ½ hearts) of damage to a player. Though a fire charge causes fire, it doesn't cause an explosion. The fire charge looks like a circular piece of coal that is glowing. You can get all the ingredients from the Nether, which is rather appropriate because, when fired from a dispenser, it looks like a blaze or ghast fireball. Consequently, the fire charge can be used to light a nether portal.

The recipe for a fire charge is shapeless. To craft a fire charge, you need blaze powder, gunpowder, and coal or charcoal (see Figure 4-3).

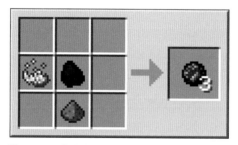

Figure 4-3: Building a fire charge.

Creating Transportation

At the point in the game where you have done most of your basic farming and mining and other survival essentials, many players have simply been walking or sprinting (requiring abundant food) everywhere they want to go. As the game progresses, especially during an adventure, a more efficient means of transportation is needed. This section can help you understand and create a vast highway.

Dangling a carrot on a stick

Until the horse was added to the game, players were forced to ride pigs. (Some still do because the sight is comical.) Here's how to ride a pig:

1. **Saddle a pig.**

   You can obtain a saddle from a dungeon, a chest, or an abandoned mineshaft or from various other places in the game.

   To put the saddle on the pig, select the saddle from the inventory and right-click on the pig. Right-click again and you'll be riding the pig. Pressing the left Shift key lets you dismount the pig.

2. **Create a carrot on a stick.**

   At some point, you'll notice that your pig just jumps up and down uncontrollably when you try to ride it. To control the pig, you must craft a carrot on a stick. The pig moves in the direction of the carrot.

To craft a carrot on a stick, place a carrot in a downward diagonal from the fishing rod, as shown in Figure 4-4. (We show you how to craft a rod in Chapter 3.) In Figure 4-5, you see an example of what the screen looks like when your character is riding a pig while holding the carrot on a stick.

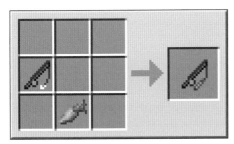

Figure 4-4: Creating a carrot on a stick with a fishing rod and a carrot.

Figure 4-5: Joseph (Thomas's brother) riding a pig.

A pig cannot swim but can climb ladders and vines. Beware: The pig slowly eats the carrot as you travel. When the carrot is gone, the pig is no longer under your control. You can right-click while holding the carrot, causing the pig to double its speed for 40 seconds at a cost of 25 percent of the carrot. While the pig is "boosting," you can switch from holding the carrot on a stick to another item (such as a weapon), allowing you to move through a mob. Though only the carrot is eaten, you must use a new fishing rod while initially crafting this item.

Rowing your boat

Boats, which are easily crafted from wooden planks, move much faster on water than players can walk. Boats float along on the current, and you can control how the boat moves by using the navigation keys on your keyboard (the W, A, S, and D keys by default). Though boats (which are essential in an Ocean biome) technically can be used on any body of water, not just the ocean, they break easily when they crash into land. Preventing a boat from crashing on land is quite difficult on lakes and rivers.

You can enter a boat from any side, including from below by right-clicking the boat, which is helpful when you're trying to surface quickly. Boats can enter the Nether if the portal is submerged at least 1 block deep in water. Some players who prefer boats to minecarts build a network of canals rather than rails. This strategy is time-consuming but effective. Doors are used to keep boats docked and to navigate canals.

Boats can be moved on land, but progress is extremely slow. Players frequently race them in water and on land in Multiplayer mode. When a boat crashes, it drops oak wood regardless of the wood used to craft the boat. (Many players use this method to convert wood.) The biggest drawback to boats is that they're fragile. Many players use them regularly only while in an Ocean biome.

To craft a boat, place 5 wood planks in the shape of the letter *U,* as shown in Figure 4-6. To ride a boat, just right-click on it.

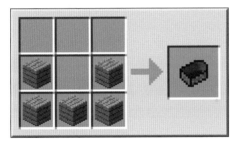

Figure 4-6: Building a boat with wood planks.

Working on the railroad

Many players navigate their worlds by creating a *track system.* When rails are placed, they automatically join together to create a straight path or a curve (when one track is joined perpendicularly to another). This strategy prevents tracks from being multidirectional unless they're connected to a redstone circuit-powered T switch.

Rails naturally attach to form either a southern or eastern orientation when placed at a cross-section, so you should plan intersections carefully. Rails can also be built to go uphill or downhill. They're regularly created with gaps or even jumps requiring impressive timing and engineering. One favorite use of rails is to create roller coaster rides (see Figure 4-7).

Figure 4-7: A roller coaster made out of rail because — hey, why not?

To craft a rail, place 6 iron ingots in 2 columns with a stick in the middle, yielding 16 pieces of rail (see Figure 4-8).

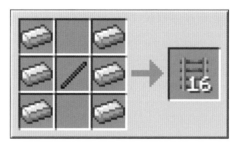

Figure 4-8: Building rail with 6 iron ingots and a stick in the middle.

Constructing a powered rail

Powered rails are used to adjust the speed of a minecart. When powered with redstone, they increase the speed while acting as a brake when turned off (except in the PE edition, which doesn't allow you to turn off powered rails). If one end of the rail is blocked, turning on a powered rail lets a stopped minecart begin moving in the nonblocked direction. Effectively, players can then load and unload carts.

Connecting powered rails doesn't continue to increase the speed of the cart significantly. Many uphill slopes require a powered rail to help minecarts successfully reach the top. Powered rails don't curve like traditional rails do.

To craft a powered rail, place a stick above a redstone in the middle column's bottom 2 boxes with 6 pieces of gold ingot in both outer columns (see Figure 4-9).

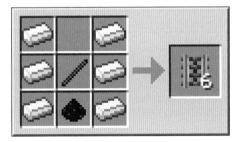

Figure 4-9: Building a powered rail with 6 pieces of gold ingot, a stick, and redstone.

Building a detector rail

When a minecart is on a *detector rail*, it gives a redstone signal to any adjacent block, including the one above and below it. A detector rail is similar to a switch that turns on things around it (by sending a redstone signal to the things around it). You can then connect a detector rail to a number of items. When a minecart travels across the detector, it activates the adjacent block using a redstone signal.

For example, connecting to a note block alerts you whenever a cart has passed, because the note block chimes. Connecting to a weapon dispenser, especially one that shoots arrows, triggers an attack on the cart (similar to a tripwire). They also can be connected to powered rails, to power several stretches of track.

To craft a detector rail, place 6 iron ingots in two vertical columns with a pressure plate in the middle and a redstone below (see Figure 4-10). This yields 6 rails.

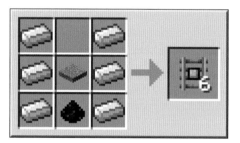

Figure 4-10: Building a detector rail.

Activating the activator rail

When a minecart passes over an *activator rail,* the contents within the cart itself are "activated" in various ways, such as the following:

- ✔ TNT is lit and exploded after a few seconds.

- ✔ A hopper is turned off and unable to load or unload.

- ✔ A player or mob is tossed from the cart (as though the Sneak command were activated).

In fact, any command block activates its sequence. Activator rails can power as many as 9 blocks on the same rail and can be connected to detector rails to power 2 separate tracks.

An activator rail is different from a detector rail in that the activator rail affects the contents of the minecart itself, whereas the detector rail only detects when the minecart passes over the rail and affects the things around the rail itself (not the minecart). So basically, if you want to affect what's in the minecart, use the activator rail. If you want to affect things on and around the rail, use the detector rail.

To craft, place 6 iron ingots in two vertical columns on the outer edges of the crafting table. Place a stick, and then a redstone torch, and then a stick in the middle column (see Figure 4-11). This yields 6 rails.

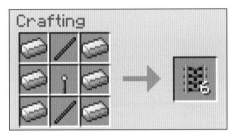

Figure 4-11: Creating an activator rail.

The engineering of rails and redstone can be difficult to understand. Many players switch to Creative mode, giving them endless inventory items, so that they can build and test their ideas. Use Creative mode as a way to practice building your redstone creations and rails.

Riding the minecart

A *minecart* is an object in Minecraft that you ride to go places fast, without running out of hunger. When you press forward on the minecart, it moves forward. A skilled player can begin pushing a minecart by walking up against the minecart (just use your W key) and then jump into it.

Using powered rails (booster rails) makes a minecart go faster, and it also starts a minecart. Mobs and villagers can ride in minecarts, and you can do other things while riding in a cart, such as shoot an arrow, use a sword, or lay track in front of the cart. Minecarts can even be merged to form a train by bumping them up against each other.

Carts lose speed over time, through turns, and when going uphill. Players receive no fall damage if the minecart falls onto tracks, so rails can be laid off a cliff with a new rail at the bottom, instead of trying to lay rail down the slope of a cliff. Players can jump from cart to cart by right-clicking.

The minecart texture is a gray, rectangular prism with a darker shade of gray for the inside texture. To craft a minecart, place 5 iron ingots — 3 on bottom and 2 on either side above the 3 you placed (see Figure 4-12).

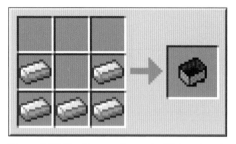

Figure 4-12: Crafting a minecart with iron ingots.

Building storage minecarts

Storage minecarts carry chests filled with items along the rails. A player cannot ride with the chest. If the minecart breaks, the chest and minecart and the contents of the chest are dropped. Many players intentionally break the minecart so that they can move it to another rail.

The biggest advantage of having a storage minecart is that you can store excess inventory in a chest and ship it to another location. The largest drawback is that the minecart with chest requires more powered rails or a powered minecart to keep it moving. Many players don't build enough powered rails in their first few attempts while working with chest minecarts.

To craft a storage minecart, place a chest and minecart onto the grid, as shown in Figure 4-13. (This recipe is shapeless and doesn't require a crafting table.)

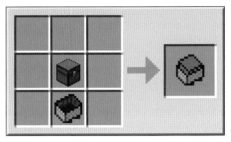

Figure 4-13: Building the shapeless minecart with chest using a chest and a minecart.

Making a minecart with a furnace

A *minecart with furnace* is essentially a train engine. It's often used to push, rather than pull, as many as 4 minecarts. You simply craft one by placing a furnace with a minecart on the crafting grid (see Figure 4-14).

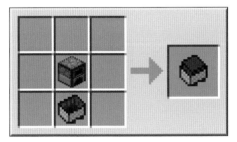

Figure 4-14: Building a powered minecart involves placing a furnace with a minecart on the crafting grid.

Just like a train in real life, after coal or charcoal is added to the furnace on the minecart (other fuel sources don't work), the cart begins to move (just hold your fuel and right-click on the furnace minecart). You simply right-click the end of the cart to indicate in which direction the cart should move. To switch directions, simply click the other end.

Powered minecarts (as they're regularly called) aren't as effective as powered rails, but they require fewer resources to build. They're of limited use going uphill. They also work much better with storage carts than with player-occupied carts. Each piece of coal lasts 3 minutes, allowing the average cart to travel 600 meters.

Crafting a minecart with hopper

A *hopper* (see the section, "Picking Up Items with a Hopper" later in this chapter to learn how to craft a hopper) picks up items and stores them in its own, internal inventory slots. When crafted with a minecart (see Figure 4-15), the hopper can move under blocks placed in mid-air, picking up items placed on top of the blocks that are within easy reach. The items can be transferred back out by placing a hopper below the track.

A hopper minecart travels much longer distances than do traditional minecarts. The hopper can be turned on and off using an activator rail.

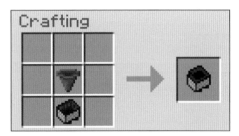

Figure 4-15: To create the minecart with hopper, place a hopper with a minecart on the crafting grid.

Exploding your way through a minecart with TNT

A minecart with TNT is a traveling bomb. A TNT minecart explodes in the following situations:

✔ **When the cart passes over an activator rail after a 4-second delay:** Incredibly, in this situation, both the rails and the blocks under the rails are unharmed by the explosion, as is the minecart, which gets dropped from you inventory.

✓ **If the cart derails and falls more than 3 blocks or if it's destroyed while moving**

✓ **If the cart catches on fire (including going through lava)**

✓ **(In some cases) while traveling around a curve if a solid block is placed beside the track:** So watch where you lay tracks.

The TNT minecart is often used as a primitive alternative to a TNT cannon. You can use it to blow up mobs from a distance, or other players in a multi-player game, or even other blocks along the way.

To craft a minecart with TNT, place the TNT and minecart into the crafting grid (see Figure 4-16).

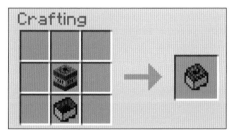

Figure 4-16: Just add TNT and a minecart to the crafting grid to make a minecart with TNT.

An activator rail prevents a hopper cart from picking up items and lights the fuse on a TNT minecart.

Engineering with Redstone

Now for our favorite part! Redstone is the "electronics" of Minecraft. If you're familiar with engineering terms, you'll find equivalents to switches, resistors, capacitors, and even transistors for performing basic logic functions. Jesse (Thomas's dad) particularly loves this stuff, because it teaches his kids all about mechanics and robotics and even electrical engineering. If you want the ultimate in STEM (Science Technology Engineering and Math) education, this section is for you!

Pressing the button

A button is the simplest switch in redstone. When you press a button, it sends a signal to an adjacent block. Wooden buttons produce a signal that lasts for 1½ seconds, and stone buttons (which are more common) produce a signal that lasts for 1 second.

When you place a button on a block, you can only place the button on an opaque area. (A button won't stick to a transparent area.) Only a player can press a button, though wooden buttons can be pressed with an arrow (which means that it can press accidentally if it's struck by a skeleton arrow, which is an extremely rare occurrence). Buttons commonly open doors, including iron doors, which cannot be opened without a redstone signal. Buttons are also common in operating dispensers.

To craft a button, place a single piece of stone or a wood planks block into the crafting grid (see Figure 4-17). Note that cobblestone and other stone materials don't work.

Wood button

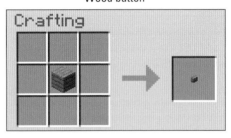

Stone button

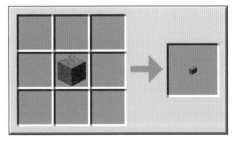

Figure 4-17: Creating wood and stone buttons.

Crafting pressure plates

A *pressure plate* is another type of switch; it sends a signal to an adjacent block or to a block that's connected to the plate via redstone wiring. When a pressure plate is connected to TNT, the result is a deadly trap. When a pressure plate is connected to a note block, the note block will create a lovely chime.

Like buttons, plates come in wood and stone. The material you use to craft your plate affects how the plate is activated:

- **Activating wooden pressure plates:** Either a player or a mob can activate a wooden plate. A player, or a mob, activates a wooden plate by stepping on the plate.

  Wooden plates can also be activated when a fishing rod's hook hits the plate, or arrows hit the plate.

  A minecart activates a wooden pressure plate when it stops on the plate, which it will do because it isn't a rail.

- **Activating stone pressure plates:** Stone pressure plates are activated only by minecarts carrying mobs or players, not by storage or furnace minecarts.

The only time a minecart doesn't stop on a pressure plate is when the cart is moving at high speed — usually, through a powered rail.

To craft a pressure plate, place 2 pieces of either wood planks or stone in a horizontal row. In Figure 4-18, you see a wood pressure plate in the making.

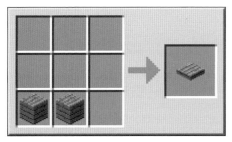

Figure 4-18: Creating a pressure plate with wood planks.

Upgrading to weighted pressure plates

This variation on pressure plates comes in light and heavy. *Light pressure plates,* made from gold, emit a signal equal only to the number of entities on it; so if a block is 4 spaces away and connected via wiring, 4 entities (blocks) would need to be dropped onto a light pressure plate to activate the block.

A *heavy pressure plate* made from iron requires 10 blocks for each level of activation. In the example, 41 blocks would need to be dropped or thrown.

Heavy pressure plates are used to activate secret doors or chests. Light pressure plates are common to activate mechanisms that you want to control and not leave up to chance by being triggered from a passing mob (like a cow wandering onto the plate).

To craft a light or heavy pressure plate, place two gold ingots for light, or two iron ingots for heavy, in a horizontal row on the crafting grid (see Figure 4-19).

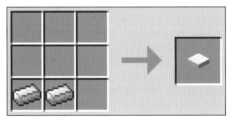

Figure 4-19: Building a heavy pressure plate using iron ingots.

Constructing trapdoors

Trapdoors on horizontal doors open when pressed or operated from a redstone signal (such as a pressure plate or button). Like doors, trapdoors prevent the flow of water and lava whether they are open or closed, and they aren't flammable. The most common use is as a trapdoor over a mining hole.

Trapdoors can be placed only on the side of a solid block and are 3/16 of a block in height.

When a trapdoor is placed on a lava block, the lava block disappears, leaving the trapdoor unharmed thus creating a path. A trapdoor also works like a path when placed on ice, allowing a player to sprint faster than a minecart.

Unlike a door, a zombie cannot destroy a trapdoor, even in Hard mode. A trapdoor is also commonly used as a trap by activating the door while a mob is standing on it.

To craft a trapdoor, place 6 wooden planks into two horizontal rows, yielding two trapdoors (see Figure 4-20).

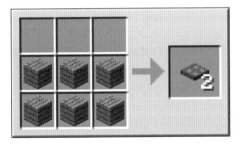

Figure 4-20: Crafting a wooden trapdoor.

Iron trapdoors require a redstone signal to open. (They don't open by simply right-clicking.) Iron trapdoors are generally used to lock items into a hole. They're crafted from 4 iron ingots placed in a square shape on the crafting grid (see Figure 4-21).

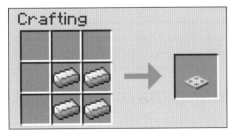

Figure 4-21: Crafting a redstone-powered iron trapdoor with 4 iron ingots.

Wooden trapdoors require 6 wooden planks and yield 2 trapdoors, whereas iron trapdoors require only 4 ingots but yield only 1 door.

Securing the proximity with a tripwire hook

A *tripwire* is a more complicated type of switch in Minecraft. Two tripwire hooks must be placed facing each other no more than 40 blocks apart. They then must be strung together with string. The string can be placed either on the ground or in the air, depending on the trap being created.

When an entity crosses the tripwire, a redstone pulse is emitted. It allows a player to place TNT (which would explode) or an arrow dispenser to discharge or perform a number of other reactions. Consider a tripwire a switch, powered by objects that cross its path.

To craft a tripwire hook, place an iron ingot on top, a stick below, and a wooden plank on the bottom (see Figure 4-22). This yields a pair of hooks.

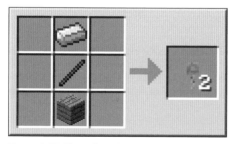

Figure 4-22: To craft a tripwire hook, you need an iron ingot, a stick, and a wooden plank placed on the crafting grid.

Protecting your inventory with a trapped chest

A *trapped chest*, which is used mostly in multiplayer games, changes a regular chest into one that emits a redstone signal when it's opened. The strength of the signal depends on the number of players opening it (1 block per player, up to 15). The trapped chest can be wired to a secret door that's accessible only when the correct number of players open the chest.

Alternatively, a trapped chest can be wired to TNT as a trap if another player is attempting to take items from the chest. Another common use is to connect a tripwire to a note block that simply alerts a player when a chest is being opened. Trapped chests can be difficult to detect. They have a slight red around the latch, which players often miss.

To craft a trapped chest, place a tripwire hook and chest in a horizontal row, as shown in Figure 4-23.

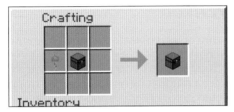

Figure 4-23: Crafting a trapped chest.

Turning on items with a lever

A *lever* is another type of redstone switch. Like a light switch, a lever stays on or off until the lever is pulled in the other direction. Unlike a common household light switch, down is On and up is Off. When a lever is placed sideways, north (or west) is On.

A lever can be wired to other items (similar to the way you wire a button or pressure plate) so that the lever activates a target block several blocks away, and a lever be placed in sequence with other levers. You can place levers on opaque blocks and on walls, floors, and ceilings. Mobs cannot turn levers.

To craft a lever, place 1 stick with 1 cobblestone directly below a stick (as shown in Figure 4-24).

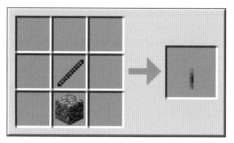

Figure 4-24: Constructing a lever with cobblestone and a stick.

Dropping inventory through the dispenser

A *dispenser* is one of the coolest redstone contraptions in Minecraft. When right-clicked, a dispenser has its own inventory, allowing you to place items inside. When activated by a redstone charge, a random item is discharged from the inventory. The selected item is random and based on stacks, not on individual items.

If a stack of 6 arrows and a stack of 3 snowballs are in the inventory, the chance is equal for arrows and snowballs, even though the inventory has twice as many arrows. Many items are simply dropped 3-x-3 blocks away. However, arrows, snowballs, fireworks, fire charges, chicken eggs, splash potions, and bottles of enchanting are shot out of the dispenser. Bombs away!

Boats and minecarts can be dispensed, but only above water and rails, respectively. Armor can also be dispensed, quickly equipping a player who is only 1 block away. Bonemeal can be dispensed automatically on a farm, improving the crops. Mob eggs can also be dispensed and consequently spawned. Also, liquids can be dispensed from buckets.

Dispensers are activated by a redstone charge running into the block or 1 block adjacent. When you place redstone wiring in a crossing pattern, 5 dispensers at a time can be triggered. A dispenser is also triggered by opening a trapped chest if the two are adjacent, so you can play fun tricks on your friends.

To craft a dispenser, place a bow (not a damaged or used bow) in the middle square with a redstone directly below. Fill the remaining 7 slots with cobblestone (not stone), as shown in Figure 4-25.

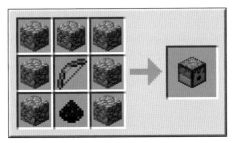

Figure 4-25: Build your dispenser with a bow, a redstone block, and cobblestone.

Building a dropper

A *dropper* works similarly to a dispenser, holding its own inventory, and is activated by a redstone circuit. It cannot dispense projectiles. (It simply drops them.) However, droppers can push items upward when they are pointed up, which is handy in pushing items up from a mine.

A dropper also puts items into other blocks that store items. For example, a dropper can place fuel into an adjacent furnace.

To craft a dropper, place a redstone in the bottom middle slot with 7 cobblestone in the other outer slots (see Figure 4-26).

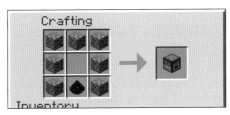

Figure 4-26: Constructing a dropper with a redstone block and 7 cobblestone blocks.

Droppers and dispensers are quite similar and look almost identical. A dispenser has a cross-shaped mouth, and a dropper has a triangle-shaped mouth.

Picking up items with a hopper

A *hopper* picks up items and stores them in its own inventory of 5 slots. It also drops items from its end. A hopper can be placed sideways, but not upside down. When connected to an item that has an inventory (such as a chest), the hopper places items directly into that inventory.

Hoppers are often used with minecarts to place items into a cart, or they be connected to a minecart and pick up items as they travel. Hoppers are also used to feed dispensers, droppers, furnaces, and brewing stands. This allows players to automate some of the work of item collection and to make traps. Hoppers are deactivated through redstone.

To craft a hopper, place 5 iron ingots in a V pattern with a chest in the center (see Figure 4-27).

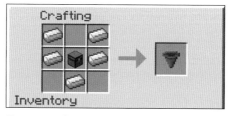

Figure 4-27: Constructing a hopper with iron ingots.

Pushing items remotely with a piston

A *piston* pushes up to 12 blocks at a time one block forward. Pistons are commonly used to open and close doors, create traps, build escalators, and combine with redstone repeaters to create logic gates (for the electronics geeks out there, yes, just like a transistor) without a redstone torch, for example. A unique feature of the piston is that it extinguishes a block that is on fire.

Despite their wooden appearance, pistons aren't flammable. You activate them using redstone. It isn't uncommon to activate a piston using a pressure plate or lever wired some distance away, which is particularly helpful in automating farms or creating mob traps.

Redstone dust and repeaters not only activate a piston directly in front of them but also power a piston below the redstone dust or repeater. Some items aren't moved by pistons, including obsidian, bedrock, blocks with extra data such as chests or furnaces, nether portals, and anvils. Items including cactus, pumpkins, jack-o'-lanterns, sugar cane, and dragon eggs are dropped when pushed. Melons and cobwebs return to slices and string, respectively. Water and lava are simply moved in their path.

Pistons also have one of the most complicated recipes. To craft, place 3 wooden planks on the top horizontal row, 4 cobblestone on both sides, an iron ingot in the middle slot, and a redstone dust in the bottom middle slot (as shown in Figure 4-28).

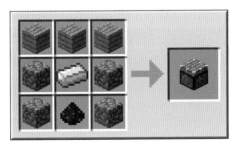

Figure 4-28: Constructing a piston with wooden planks, cobblestone, iron ingot, and redstone dust.

Constructing a sticky piston

A sticky piston operates the same as a piston but also pulls blocks in addition to pushing them. The same rules apply in pulling blocks as in pushing them. A sticky piston cannot pull a block back if it pushed the block over a hole. (The block will fall.) Similarly, sticky pistons cannot hold sand and gravel horizontally.

To craft a sticky piston, place a slimeball on top of a piston in the crafting grid, as shown in Figure 4-29.

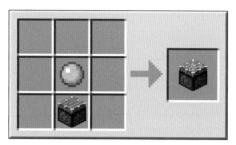

Figure 4-29: Building a sticky piston using a piston and a slimeball.

Detecting light with a daylight sensor

A *daylight sensor* works like a solar panel and emits a redstone signal during daylight hours, giving you a way to identify whether it's light outside. If an opaque block is placed above the sensor, it emits, at random, only a weak signal or no signal (but usually no signal). During midday, the sensor can power up to 15 blocks but only 5 during evening or morning hours.

Right-clicking the sensor will change it into a night sensor. This allows a player to automatically turn on redstone lamps at night, which will prevent mobs from spawning and grow crops.

When mining (where daylight isn't obvious), a sensor can be connected to a redstone signal to warn a player when it's nearly nighttime. Both rain and thunderstorms weaken the signal strength of the sensor. Sensors only work by sunlight, and not by other light sources such as torches.

To craft a daylight sensor, place 3 glass blocks (not panes – see Chapter 5) on the top horizontal row, 3 nether quartz (see Chapter 3) on the middle row, and 3 wood slabs (see Chapter 1) on the bottom row (as shown in Figure 4-30).

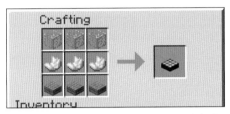

Figure 4-30: Building a daylight sensor with glass blocks, nether quartz, and wood slabs.

Powering the lights with a redstone torch

A *redstone torch,* which is the primary power source in red-stone circuitry, provides constant power to wires, doors, and other objects and is used extensively as an inverter in circuits and logic gates. A redstone torch is turned off when the block it's placed on receives power from another redstone source, and it's activated using a switch or whenever it receives (or loses) a signal from a powered wire. Think of it performing the opposite of the power it is receiving (when it receives a signal, it turns off. When it loses the signal, it turns on).

When a redstone torch powers a wire, the signal can be car-ried 15 blocks away and can operate pistons, switches, and doors, for example. Redstone torches are commonly used to activate traps and mechanisms and can open locked iron doors. Redstone torches produce half the light of traditional torches, making them ineffective at preventing mob spawns. They're also critical ingredients in activator rails, redstone comparators, and redstone repeaters.

To craft a redstone torch, place a redstone dust in the center and a stick directly below the redstone dust (see Figure 4-31).

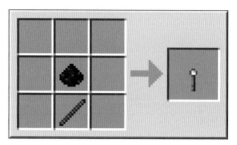

Figure 4-31: Building a redstone torch with a redstone dust and a stick.

Lighting the way with a redstone lamp

A *redstone lamp* is one step brighter than a torch (luminance 15) but glows only when constantly powered, which lets it be turned on and off (usually, from a switch). The lamp is brown when off and gold when lit. This type of lamp is mostly used to decorate, but can be effective in mob traps and mushroom farming.

To craft a redstone lamp, place a glowstone in the center slot with 4 redstone surrounding it (see Figure 4-32).

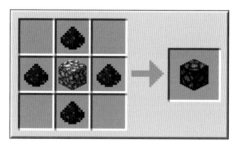

Figure 4-32: Crafting a redstone lamp with a glowstone and redstone.

Extending power with a redstone repeater

As we describe in the earlier section "Powering the lights with a redstone torch," a redstone torch can power items as far as 15 blocks away. A redstone repeater renews a redstone signal back to full strength, allowing for longer circuits than the typical 15 blocks. It has a back and a front, with an arrow pointing toward the front. The arrow tells you which way the repeater is facing, so you know which is front, and which is back.

A repeater's signal is strong enough to power through an opaque block and onto an adjacent redstone component. Redstone repeaters have a built-in delay of 1 redstone tick, but can be right-clicked to increase the delay to 4. Because a repeater has a front and a back, it can transmit a signal in only one direction. A repeater can also be locked, preventing it from transmitting a signal by placing another repeater or comparator facing its side. Also, a repeater can be placed only on an opaque block such as dirt.

A redstone repeater can be crafted by placing redstone in the center of the crafting grid, 2 redstone torches on either side of the redstone, and 3 stones of any type in the 3 slots at the bottom of the grid. Figure 4-33 shows a grid with these items.

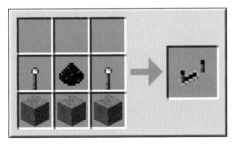

Figure 4-33: Creating a redstone repeater with redstone torches, redstone, and stone.

Determining logic with a redstone comparator

A *redstone comparator* is similar to a repeater except that it has an additional input from the side. There are different modes for the comparator depending on the front torch. When the front torch is lit, the comparator subtracts the side input from the back input to determine the strength of the output signal. The back input must be larger than the side input or else the comparator doesn't fire (similarly to a transistor).

After right-clicking, the front torch goes dark and the output signal is the full strength of the back input if the back signal exceeds the side. The comparator also has a 1 redstone tick delay. When a comparator is placed by a block with an inventory (such as a chest), the output of the comparator is based on the amount of used inventory space in the block.

To craft a redstone comparator, place 1 redstone torch in the top middle of the crafting grid, and 2 more on each side of the middle row. Place a nether quartz in the middle, and place 3 of any stone at the bottom of the crafting grid (see Figure 4-34).

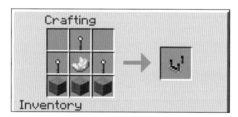

Figure 4-34: Building a redstone comparator with 3 redstone torches, a nether quartz, and 3 stones of any type.

Sounding the alarm with a note block

The *note block*, which is a musical block, works when activated by redstone. It plays a single note even when fed a continuous signal. Notes can be heard as far as 48 blocks away, which allows a player to use a note block as a signal.

Multiple note blocks can be placed to make a song or chord. When a note block plays, a colored note flies out the top of it. A note block is set up by pitch and instrument. To create the pitch, right-click on the note block as many as 24 times, each time raising the pitch by half a step. The note color changes with the pitch, starting with green and moving through yellow, orange, red, purple, blue, and, finally, a myriad of green shades. Two full octaves of notes are available.

To pick the instrument, place the note block on top of various blocks, as indicated in Table 4-1.

Table 4-1	Instrument Types
When You Place a Note Block on This Type of Block . . .	*. . . You Get This Instrument*
Wood	Bass guitar
Sand or gravel	Snare drum
Glass or glowstone	Clicks/sticks
Stone, including obsidian, netherrack, and bricks	Bass drum
Other types	Piano/harp

Note blocks need at least 1 block of air above them in order to sound. Though a variety of redstone circuits power the note block, switches are often so loud that the note cannot be heard. On the other hand, redstone repeaters simplify the process of activating multiple note blocks to create a melody.

To craft a note block, place 8 wood blocks (of any type, as long as they're wood) around a single redstone in the middle (as shown in Figure 4-35).

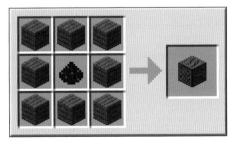

Figure 4-35: A note block requires 8 wood blocks around a single redstone block.

Designing fireworks with a firework star

The firework star determines the color, effect, and shape of a firework rocket. Color is determined by the dye that's added to the star recipe (as explained in Chapter 7), including a combination of dyes. Adding dye to an existing star adds a fade-to-color dimension.

The basic recipe for a firework star is gunpowder and dye (see Figure 4-36). You can learn more about gunpower in Chapter 9. Find out about dye in Chapter 7.

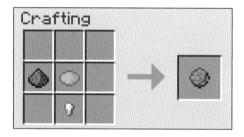

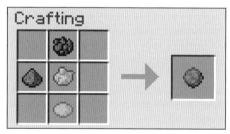

Figure 4-36: The firework star can work with optional ingredients and with dyes.

This recipe can be enhanced to add effect and shape. The effect can be either trail or twinkle or both; see Table 4-2.

Table 4-2	Firework Effects
Effect	**Recipe**
Trail	Add 1 diamond to recipe.
Twinkle	Add 1 glowstone dust (see Chapter 5 to learn more about glowstone and glowstone dust).
Trail and twinkle	And 1 diamond and 1 glowstone.

Minecraft has 5 shape options, but only 1 shape option can be selected per star, as defined in Table 4-3.

Table 4-3	Firework Shapes
Shape	**Recipe**
Small ball	It's the default size.
Large ball	Add 1 fire charge to crafting recipe.
Burst	Add 1 feather.
Star	Add 1 gold nugget.
Creeper	Add any head (usually obtained in Creative mode).

A firework star can have one effect, both effects, or no effect, but it can have only one shape.

With the exception of the wither skeleton, which is rarely dropped, all other mob heads can be obtained only in Creative mode. The mob heads available are the skeleton, wither skeleton, zombie, player, and creeper.

Launching the firework rocket

A firework rocket's color, shape, and effect are based solely on the star that's used to craft it. When a star isn't used, the firework rocket simply has a rocket trail with no impressive firework explosion (see Figure 4-37 to see the difference). The number of gunpowder used to craft the rocket determines the flight duration, with a maximum of 3 per rocket.

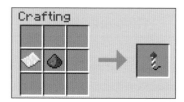
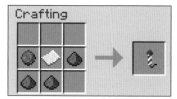

Figure 4-37: A firework's color, shape, and effect are based solely on the star that's used to craft it. When a star isn't used, the firework rocket simply has a rocket trail with no impressive firework explosion.

A firework doesn't destroy a block, even if it explodes on top of the block. Rockets also explode underwater, looking identical to how they explode in the air. If a firework hits a block, it explodes above the block after a delay, explodes on contact above the block, or continues at a new angle and explodes normally. Fireworks can be launched by right-clicking or using a dispenser.

Spawning items using the nether reactor core

The *nether reactor core,* a block that's unique to the PE (Pocket Edition) (and Pi, or Raspberry Pi Edition) version of Minecraft, is primarily used to create the nether reactor. The nether reactor spawns a variety of items in several seconds, providing a player with an extensive set of items, and it's the only way to obtain glowstone and nether quartz while playing in Survival mode.

To craft the nether reactor core, place 3 diamonds in the center vertical column with 6 iron ingots in the outer two columns, as shown in the PE edition grid in Figure 4-38.

Figure 4-38: To create a reactor core, you need 3 diamonds and 6 iron ingots.

5

Expanding Your House

In This Chapter

- Crafting advanced household items
- Understanding items with powers
- Expanding houses and bases
- Crafting items from the Nether and the End

*M*any players have established successful farms and mines, including redstone contraptions to help automate their farms. These players have long since mastered the basics of building a simple shelter with a bed and chests. They have upgraded their tools, swords, and armor, and they have used various forms of transportation to explore the biome. If you are one of these players, you're ready to transform a simple shelter into a wealthy mansion and to create bases.

Additionally, you may have begun to advance to the Nether and the End (which ironically, is not the end of the game). Many useful and decorative items can be crafted only from materials gathered in these other dimensions.

To get you started, you can craft various items to make your Minecraft house a home. Take advantage of these items to make your game experience more comfortable, and more advantageous as you progress.

Climbing with Ladders

The main purpose of a *ladder* is to provide access up or down without the space and design of a staircase. Ladders can be placed next to each other to connect two blocks. To hold on to a ladder, press the Sneak (Shift) command while you're on the ladder. This action prevents you from falling off.

On a ladder, you have a maximum climbing speed, including climbing down. If you're falling and you land on a ladder, you naturally slow down to climbing speed and avoid fall damage.

Ladders are lava resistant and cannot be burned as fuel, despite being made of wood. Because they're inflammable, they can be used in place of glass as the ceiling of your house and still allow lava light to shine through. Ladders are also water resistant and create air pockets wherever you place them.

To make three ladders, place 7 sticks to form an H on the crafting grid — 3 vertically on each side and 1 in the middle (see Figure 5-1).

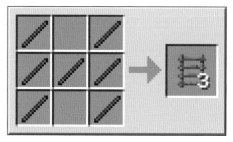

Figure 5-1: Crafting a ladder.

Messaging with Signs

The main purpose of a *sign* in Minecraft is for players to leave messages for each other in a multiplayer game, including the rules for an adventure map. Also, a sign is a nonsolid block and, just like a door, can therefore stop the flow of liquids. You can also use a sign as a decorative item, such as a headboard with your name inscribed.

Each sign holds 4 lines of text with as many as 15 characters per line. You cannot edit the text after a sign is complete. Neither does the copy-and-paste action work on signs. Parents can take comfort! Minecraft doesn't allow inappropriate language — it checks before allowing a sign to be posted, though this method is not perfect (and only applies to multiplayer mode). For example, the words *hoe, monster,* and *shaft* aren't allowed, even though they apply to the game.

You can change the color of text by using a map editor like MCEdit. Map editors allow players to alter portions of the game, like terrain or even inventory.

To change the text, you can break a sign and post a new one. When you break a sign, a sword is effective but takes double damage.

You can place a sign in the ground or on a wall or block. When placed underwater, a sign creates an air bubble, allowing you to breathe. Additionally, mobs can walk through signs, though they usually see them as solid and try to walk over them. When you place signs on the edge of a cliff, mobs often try to walk over them and fall off instead.

To craft signs, place 6 wood planks on the top 2 rows with a stick in the bottom middle slot. Each recipe yields 3 signs (see Figure 5-2).

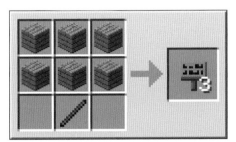

Figure 5-2: Crafting 3 signs with 6 wood planks and a stick.

Banners

Banners work much like signs and hold a flag. They can be placed on the wall or on the ground facing different directions. A basic banner is crafted using wool and a stick taking on the color of the wool (16 different color possibilities).

Banners are customized using a complex set of recipes with a maximum of 6 different layers to create the final design. Each layer cannot be uncrafted but can be removed one layer at a time in a cauldron. To craft, place 6 wool in the top two horizontal rows with a stick in the bottom middle slot, as shown in Figure 5-3.

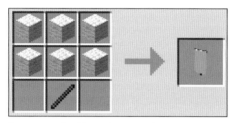

Figure 5-3: Crafting a banner with wool and a stick.

Decorating with Flowerpots

The *flowerpot* is a decorative block that allows you to plant plants 1 block high, including certain flowers, saplings, mushrooms (which can be found on the mob mooshroom; see Chapter 3), and cacti. When saplings and cacti are planted, neither will grow, allowing you to "store" those plants. Also, when cacti are in flowerpots, they don't injure players or destroy items.

To craft a flowerpot, place 3 bricks (made by smelting clay; see Chapter 6) in a V pattern, as shown in Figure 5-4.

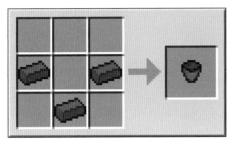

Figure 5-4: Crafting a flowerpot.

Utilizing Paper

Paper is of no use in and of itself but is an ingredient in crafting other items, including maps, fireworks, and books. You cannot write on paper by itself.

To craft, place 3 sugar canes in a horizontal row. Each recipe yields 3 papers (see Figure 5-5).

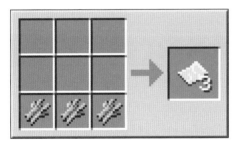

Figure 5-5: Making paper with sugar cane.

Enchanting with Books

Books are necessary ingredients in enchantment tables and bookshelves (see Chapter 8). You craft a book by using a shapeless recipe consisting of 3 papers and 1 leather (see Figure 5-6). Leather can be acquired by killing cows and drops in quantities of 0-2 leather per cow. In the PE version, only 3 paper are needed to craft a book.

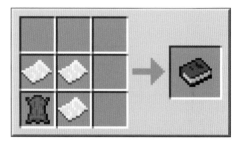

Figure 5-6: Crafting books in both the PC and PE editions of Minecraft.

Writing Stories with a Book and Quill

A book in Minecraft can be 50 pages long and have as many as 256 characters per page. After you craft a book, you can write in the book using the book-and-quill recipe. You can write a few pages and then save the book until later in the inventory.

When the book is complete, you sign it so that a title is created and the book bears your name. You can rename a book only by using an anvil. After the book is signed, however, you cannot edit it.

Books are used largely for two reasons:

- ✔ To write messages, record a diary, or explain an adventure map
- ✔ To trade for emeralds (at a 1:1 ratio)

Though you can write a book using copy-and-paste, the text must be less than 1 Minecraft page (roughly 256 characters).

To craft, place the following anywhere in the grid, as shown in Figure 5-7: a book, a feather (often dropped when you kill a chicken), and an ink sac (dropped when you kill a squid, or sometimes found when fishing).

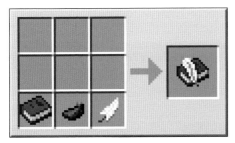

Figure 5-7: Crafting the book and quill so that you can write in your book.

You can copy and stack an entire book into the inventory. The copy, often called a *written book,* lets you make multiple copies to distribute to other players (especially for an adventure map) or to create a stack to trade for emeralds. To copy a book, place a regular book and the book-with-quill that is to be copied anywhere on the crafting grid, creating two books (see Figure 5-8).

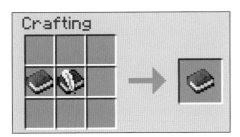

Figure 5-8: Copying a book on the crafting grid.

Building a Bookshelf

A *bookshelf* is used to reach the higher levels of enchantment by using an enchantment table. To reach the maximum enchanting level, you must craft 15 bookshelves.

When a bookshelf is placed near an enchantment table, glyph particles fly from the bookshelf to the table (see Chapter 8). The bookshelf has a wooden look on top and bottom, and the look of various books stacked on shelves on its 4 sides.

Each shelf requires 3 books and 6 wooden planks to craft (with the 3 books on the center horizontal row). Each book requires paper and leather, which in turn were crafted from sugar cane (and, possibly, rabbit hide, which becomes available in the 1.8 update of the game). Each bookshelf therefore requires 9 sugar cane, 3 leather (12 rabbit hide or 3 dropped cow leather), and 1.5 blocks of wood (see Figure 5-9).

Bookshelves catch fire easily!

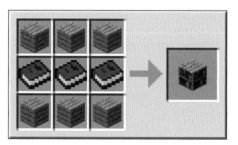

Figure 5-9: Building the bookshelf.

Navigating with an Empty Map

When a map is created and then right-clicked into your hand, it becomes a map centered at that location. As you explore with map in hand (as opposed to in your inventory), the map draws itself. A map is specific to where it was first activated, such as the overworld, Nether, or End, and it remains centered on that activation point.

Maps are largely used in the overworld to give you a sense of direction when you're lost and to show important landmarks, including mineral deposits, sand, or lava. Maps can also be shared with other players. Maps in the Nether have only a red-and-gray pattern showing your location compared to the center, where the map would have first been activated.

To create an empty map, place 8 pieces of paper around a compass in the center square (see Figure 5-10). The next section explains how to craft a compass.

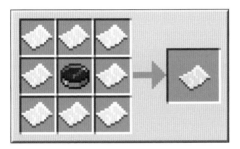

Figure 5-10: Creating an empty map.

Orienting with a Compass

The *compass* points to your original spawning point. Even if you sleep in a bed, altering your respawning point, the compass needle continues to point to the original spawning point. A compass works in the inventory or in a chest, and even when held by another player. The exception is that a compass does not work in the Nether or the End. A compass is also an ingredient in crafting a blank map.

To craft a compass, place a redstone in the center square with 4 iron ingots surrounding it, one in each direction (see Figure 5-11).

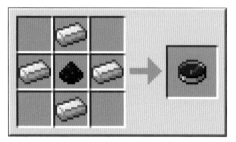

Figure 5-11: Crafting a compass.

Telling the Time with a Clock

The *clock,* sometimes referred to as a *watch,* tells you when it is day and when it is night — which is particularly helpful in a cave because you can sleep during the night and prevent mobs from spawning. A clock can even be placed in an item frame, creating a wall clock. Like a compass, the clock tells time if left on the ground or in a chest, or even midway through crafting. However, clocks don't work in the Nether or the End. Because a clock uses a significant amount of gold, many players choose not to craft one.

To craft a clock, place 1 redstone in the center of the crafting grid with 4 gold ingots, one in each direction around the redstone (see Figure 5-12).

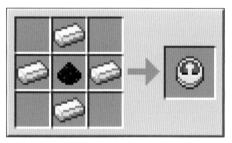

Figure 5-12: Making a clock.

Xbox 360 rewards you with a miniature wristwatch after you complete 100 day/night cycles.

Hanging Paintings

Paintings are placed on flat, vertical surfaces and expand, to the best they can, to fit particular areas. Paintings are randomly generated from a database of work from (primarily) the artist Kristoffer Zetterstrand.

A painting, which is inflammable, protects the block on which it's placed. When a painting is hit by most objects (such as snowballs), it's knocked off but not destroyed. Because it's knocked off easily, it rarely hides secret doors — but can hide chests.

Place paintings carefully — a painting isn't a block, but rather an entity allowing mobs and players to walk through and allowing light to shine through.

A painting is crafted with 8 pieces of stick surrounding a wool item in the center slot (see Figure 5-13). The color of wool has no influence on the random painting that is created.

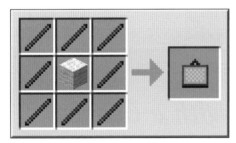

Figure 5-13: Making a painting to hang on a wall.

Storing with an Item Frame

An *item frame* holds items and blocks and can be placed on any solid blocks, trees, fences, cobblestone walls, or pressure plates. To place an item into the frame, simply right-click while holding the item.

Frames can hold maps, clocks, compasses, or books, for example, which frees up storage space in the inventory and allows for easy reference. Though item frames can hold illuminated blocks such as lava or glowstone, those blocks no longer glow while in the frame. Frames are commonly used for maps because they show markers for other frames containing maps. You can turn items within a frame at 45 degree angles by right-clicking the frame.

Depending on the angle, the frame emits a redstone signal that can be read by a comparator. Frames are occasionally used to color code levers by placing dyed wool in the frame and then hanging the frame on the lever. Most importantly, you can clone items in Creative mode by placing multiple copies of the same item into different frames, which is particularly useful for copying enchanted items.

To craft an item frame, place 8 sticks around a leather in the center square (see Figure 5-14).

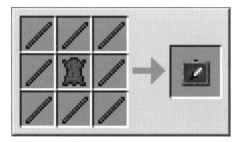

Figure 5-14: Building an item frame.

Signaling with a Beacon

A *beacon* is one of the most-often-used objects without enchantment. It provides not only light (though plenty of other objects, such as torches, do that) but also status effect to players. Status effects are similar to superpowers. Table 5-1 outlines the basic status effects.

Table 5-1		Basic Status Effects
Icon	**Effect**	**How the Effect Helps Your Player**
🐾	Speed	Increased movement
⛏	Haste	Increased mining speed

Icon	Effect	How the Effect Helps Your Player
	Resistance	Increased armor strength
	Jump boost	Increased jumping height and distance
	Strength	Increased damage
	Regeneration	Restores health points

For a beacon to activate these powers, you must place it on a pyramid. The smallest pyramid is a 9-block group placed on a single 3 x 3 layer with the beacon placed on the middle block. The largest pyramid, which is 4 layers high, consists of 164 blocks with a 9 x 9 layer on the bottom. You can make pyramids from iron, gold, diamond, or emerald blocks, including a combination of each block. Only the height of a pyramid matters, so you gain no advantage by using more-expensive blocks to construct a pyramid.

After you construct a pyramid with a beacon placed on top (see Figure 5-15), the beacon must be fueled with an iron or gold ingot or a piece of diamond or emerald. To fuel or "feed" the beacon, right-click the beacon block and the beacon's GUI will appear. Simply place the mineral of choice in the GUI and it will be fed.

Figure 5-15: The beacon, when placed on the pyramid.

After you fuel the beacon, you select a status effect (see Figure 5-16). However, regeneration is available in only the tallest pyramid, and it's a secondary status that's chosen in addition to another status from the list.

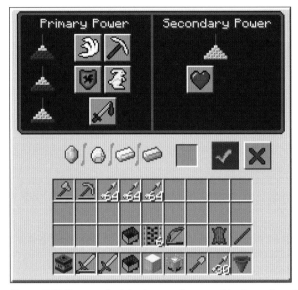

Figure 5-16: You can fuel the beacon in a graphical user interface (GUI).

The beacon's power grows a larger radius based on the height of the pyramid. A taller pyramid lets you be farther away and still benefit from the status effect. A beacon is often placed in a lower spot because its effects go upward as well as outward. A beacon also produces a light stream upward, making it a powerful landmark.

A beacon works, however, only if it has an unobstructed view of the sky (in the overland or End) or has transparent blocks above it (with the exception of water). The only downside to using a beacon lies in the difficulty of creating it. The beacon itself requires rare obsidian and enough mined mineral to create the pyramid.

The light of a beacon can now change color by placing stained glass in the light beam (at its source on the top of the beacon or higher in the sky). Because you can stack multiple stained glass, the color combinations are almost infinite.

To craft a beacon, place 3 obsidian on the bottom horizontal row, a nether star (dropped when you kill the 3-headed wither mob) in the center, and glass (not glass panes – see Chapter 5) in the remaining 5 slots (see Figure 5-17).

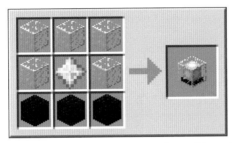

Figure 5-17: Making a beacon on the crafting grid.

Crafting on an Anvil

An anvil is useful in Minecraft to repair items without breaking the enchantment. An anvil can also combine enchantments and rename items. An anvil is more complicated than a crafting table, and it requires experience points (earned by completing tasks in the game, and by killing mobs) and materials in order to repair an item. Like many of the items an anvil repairs — including tools, weapons, and armor — an anvil becomes damaged with use and lasts, on average, for only 24 uses. After you craft an anvil, it opens its own menu when you right-click it (see Figure 5-18).

To repair or enchant an item, follow these steps:

1. **Place the item in the first slot.**
2. **Place the sacrifice piece in the second slot.**

   For enchantments, you place the enchantment book in the second slot. For other items, you place an ingredient (such as iron ingot to repair an iron sword) in the second slot.

   The game calculates the cost of the repair and determines whether you have enough experience points (seen as the bottom bar below the hearts) to complete the repair. (This statement does not apply to Creative mode.) Repairing on an anvil is generally only desirable to preserve enchantments.

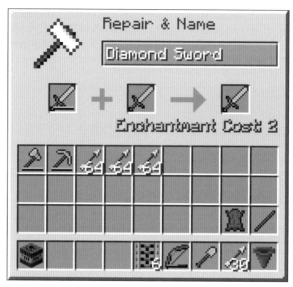

Figure 5-18: Right-clicking the anvil pulls up the Repair & Name inventory screen.

You can drop an anvil and inflict considerable damage on mobs and players (the anvil will not be damaged).

An anvil is one of the more expensive items to craft, because it requires more iron than a complete set of iron armor. To craft an anvil, place 3 blocks of iron on the top horizontal row, 3 iron ingots on the bottom horizontal row, and 1 iron ingot in the middle square (see Figure 5-19). Then you have a total of 31 iron ingots (because blocks are composed of 9 iron ingots apiece).

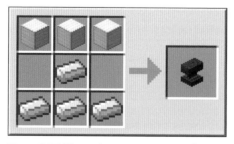

Figure 5-19: The recipe to create an anvil.

Sharing with an Ender Chest

An ender chest holds items just like normal chests, but shares that inventory with other ender chests that are placed anywhere, including in other dimensions such as the Nether or the End (the inventory is only available to the player who created the chest). When an ender chest is broken, its items do not drop. You can retrieve them at another ender chest or by creating a new ender chest.

You can then stockpile items that are easily accessible at all bases or houses. Though ender chests are explosion-resistant, you can break them with a pickaxe or enderdragon.

Ender chests don't work with hoppers, droppers, command blocks, or pistons. They're treated as inventory of the player and not as a block.

The only downside is that an ender chest is far more difficult to make than a chest, requiring 9 blocks of obsidian and an eye of ender. You see the recipe for an ender chest in Figure 5-20. Obsidian can be mined at places where water meets lava throughout the game. It can also be obtained on the Nether Portal (in the Nether), or in unlimited form in The End region on the platform that is created each time you enter The End. The next section explains how to create an eye of ender.

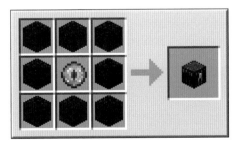

Figure 5-20: Making an ender chest.

Seeing through the Eye of Ender

Eye of ender is used to locate end portals and as the final ingredient in crafting an ender chest. To locate an end portal, simply hold and right-click the eye to send it into the sky, toward the portal, with a trail of purple dust to follow. After you find a portal, 12 eyes are needed to activate it.

To craft the eye of ender, place blaze powder (see Chapter 8) and an ender pearl (dropped by Endermen when they die) anywhere on the grid (see Figure 5-21).

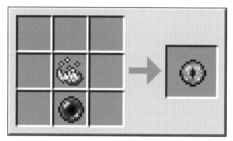

Figure 5-21: Making an eye of ender.

Using Glass

To create glass, which can be turned into glass panes for a more effective window, simply place sand or red sand in a furnace and — *voilà!* — you've made glass (see Figure 5-22).

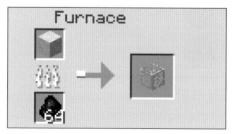

Figure 5-22: Making glass in the furnace.

Dealing with Glass Panes

A special property of glass panes is that, when they aren't connected to anything, they look like a plus sign (+) when viewed from the top, but become flat (-) when placed next to other blocks. Glass panes are used to create air pockets in water and lava. They are more efficient than glass when used in a house. Players can walk through glass panes (be careful when you use them on a hillside cliff!), but they're also watertight, so they're useful in underwater construction.

Glass pains — er, panes — are just not a fan-favorite texture. Folks complain that the glass isn't see-through or just looks terrible. We can live with the texture, but it's not the best in the game. The texture of the glass panes is a border with diagonal blue-and-gray lines.

To craft glass panes, place 6 glass blocks in the bottom two rows of the crafting grid (see Figure 5-23). Crafting this way gives you 16 panes.

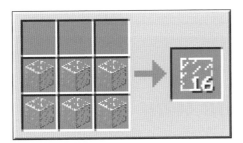

Figure 5-23: Crafting glass panes.

Carving a Jack-o'-Lantern

Glowing in all directions and much brighter than torches (a jack-o'-lantern has a light level of 15, vs. a torch's light level of 14), jack-o'-lanterns glow underwater and cause snow and ice to melt. They're similar to sea lanterns, glowstone, and beacons, but are easier to obtain.

You can place jack-o'-lanterns on a solid or opaque block (except for TNT), and they remain there even if the supporting block is removed.

A common light source for crops and underwater exploration, jack-o'-lanterns are used to light trails in the Nether because jack-o'-lanterns resist ghast bombs. You can use jack-o'-lanterns in place of pumpkins to create snow golems or iron golems. A jack-o'-lantern has a face side but emits light equally in all directions. Unlike a pumpkin, a jack-o'-lantern cannot be worn as a mask.

To craft a jack-o'-lantern, place 1 pumpkin above a torch (see Figure 5-24).

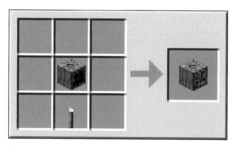

Figure 5-24: Making a jack-o'-lantern on the crafting grid with a pumpkin and torch.

Lighting the Way with Glowstone

Glowstone is a transparent block. Equivalent to a jack-o'-lantern with a light level of 15, glowstone works underwater and melts snow and ice. However, glowstone is found only in the Nether and is often broken to create dust for brewing recipes and fireworks. You may want to store the dust in blocks for use in brewing (see Chapter 8).

Here are a few common uses for glowstone:

✔ Provide light for crops.

✔ Guide boats through the water.

✔ Create a redstone lamp or a block in redstone logic-gate designs. (See Chapter 4.)

✔ Send a one-way signal (by placing glowstone next to redstone).

To craft glowstone, place 4 glowstone dust in the lower-left corner of the crafting grid (see Figure 5-25). You find glowstone dust in the Nether.

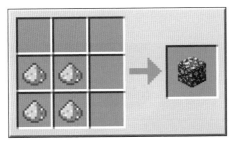

Figure 5-25: Making glowstone with glowstone dust from the Nether.

Letting It Snow

You can craft a full-size snow block from 4 snowballs (obtained when a snow block is destroyed with a shovel) placed in a square pattern (see Figure 5-26). Though this recipe cannot be reversed, you can store snow blocks in the inventory and break it with a shovel to retrieve the snowballs.

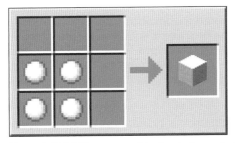

Figure 5-26: Making a snow block out of snowballs.

Snowballs are useful in herding and knocking back mobs without doing damage. (Snowballs damage the Blaze and enderdragon.) Though snow blocks don't melt from lava, fire, torches, or water, they collapse in an explosion. Used to build fortresses in taiga and tundra biomes, snow blocks are also used to create snow golems.

Snow golems make a player-created mob that is allied with the player. They throw snowballs at enemy mobs and leave a trail of snow that you can harvest. Snow golems technically are not crafted but are created by placing two snow blocks on the ground (not on a crafting grid) and then placing a pumpkin (not a jack-o'-lantern) on top (see Figure 5-27).

Figure 5-27: Creating your own army of snow golems.

Weaving White Wool

Wool can be crafted from string, but string cannot be crafted or obtained by breaking wool. Because string is a necessary ingredient in several recipes — including bows, leads, and fishing rods — you're extremely unlikely to use the recipe to craft string into wool. You obtain string by killing spiders, which can be difficult.

Wool is much more easily obtained directly by shearing or killing sheep. Although wool is naturally white, you can easily dye it (see Chapter 7). Wool is extremely useful in the game but is practically never obtained by crafting.

If you must craft wool (vs. shearing or killing sheep, which is easier), place 4 string in a square configuration (see Figure 5-28).

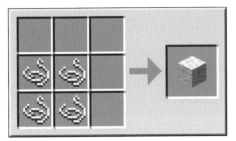

Figure 5-28: Crafting wool from string.

Building Iron Bars

Iron bars are used somewhat like fences or glass panes but are only 1 block high. They're often placed next to a door so that you can shoot arrows between the bars. (Otherwise, iron bars work as a solid block.) Iron bars are also used as nether windows because they're blast-resistant and block a ghast's sight.

You can slip through the bars in a 2 x 2 area, but because they prevent water from flowing through them, they can be used as an underwater door. Iron bars can also contain a fire.

Another use for iron bars is speeding up the healing of a zombie villager (the most common hostile mob, which can be "cured," turning them into a normal villager). Placing bars close to the villager will speed up their healing process.

To craft iron bars, place 6 iron ingots into two horizontal rows, to yield an astonishing 16 bars (see Figure 5-29).

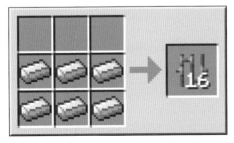

Figure 5-29: Building iron bars with iron ingots.

Playing a Jukebox

A *jukebox* plays music discs. You can find music discs in dungeon chests or when a skeleton's arrow kills a creeper. Many players create a mob trap by placing both skeletons and creepers in the same trap.

Minecraft has 12 discs. A music disc can play only once before you have to take it out of the jukebox and reinsert it. The sound from a jukebox travels roughly 65 blocks (more than a note block). At the top of a jukebox is a slot where you insert the music disc, and the sides have the same texture as note blocks.

The recipe requires a diamond, in honor of the diamond-tipped phonograph (or record player). To craft a jukebox, place a diamond in the center slot with wooden planks in the other 8 spaces (see Figure 5-30).

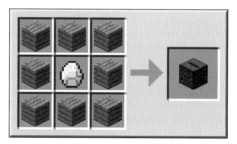

Figure 5-30: Making a jukebox to play music.

6
Crafting with Decorative Blocks

In This Chapter

▶ Making all sorts of decorative blocks

▶ Creating new prismarine blocks

▶ Soaking and drying sponges

*M*any blocks in Minecraft are largely decorative, with few practical uses. They enhance the creativity and visual effects of the game and allow players to design custom homes and ornate bases.

Many decorative blocks involve multiple steps, including furnace and crafting recipes. Decorative items greatly enhance the creative side of the gameplay, but can be time consuming. Many players may want to switch to Peaceful mode or Creative mode while exploring these blocks.

Placing Slabs

All stone blocks in Minecraft can be crafted into slabs. *Slabs* are half-blocks and can be placed upside-down, in order to put things, such as redstone, underneath them (slabs only take up ½ block space, meaning there is an empty space between them and the adjacent blocks around them). To place a slab upside-down, choose one of these methods:

- Right-click on the bottom of a ceiling block and remove the ceiling block.
- Right-click on the top half of a block to place the slab connecting to the top of that block.

Slabs offer differing damage values (the difficulty level of being able to break one, or durability), presented in this list from lowest to highest:

- Stone
- Sandstone
- Cobblestone
- Bricks
- Stone bricks
- Wood
- Nether brick
- Quartz

Upside-down slabs have a greater damage value than those placed in the bottom position. Slabs aren't shown as solid blocks when interacting with redstone, which allows you to place a wire above or below a slab without interruption.

Interestingly, on upside-down slabs, redstone placed on top can transmit signals only going upward (not downward), and it can receive signals from 1 block below. Upside-down slabs can then be used as redstone ladders. Slabs are also highly blast resistant, allowing them to be placed below TNT to mitigate the damage or to limit the damage from exploding creepers. Slabs are also commonly used as stairs. To craft a slab, place 3 blocks of the same material in a horizontal row to yield 6 slabs (see Figure 6-1).

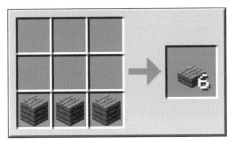

Figure 6-1: Crafting a slab from any 3 blocks of the same stone material.

In Release 1.8 of Minecraft, you can craft the following materials into stone slabs using the same recipe:

- ✔ Andesite

- ✔ Diorite

- ✔ Granite

- ✔ Polished andesite

- ✔ Polished diorite

- ✔ Polished granite

You can make wooden slabs only by using blocks of the same type of wood (unlike other wooden objects), and they retain the name of that wood, such as oak slab or birch slab.

Many types of slabs can be crafted to form the chiseled version of that block, creating incredible visual effects. For example, 2 stone brick slabs can be crafted into a chiseled stone brick. This chapter spells out these recipes.

Climbing Stairs

The purpose of stairs is to let players climb without jumping. Though slabs can be laid in a stair pattern, actual stairs are more compact and allow for a steeper climb. You can make stairs from the same materials as slabs; wooden stairs must be made exclusively from one type of wooden plank (spruce or jungle, for example). Redstone wires can run under a staircase, hiding the wires from view without disrupting the signal.

Stairs can be placed upside-down (usually, to make arches), and wooden stairs are flammable. Water flows down stairs, creating a transport system.

To craft stairs, place 6 items of the same type (wooden planks, brick, or quartz, for example) in a stair pattern to yield 4 stairs (see Figure 6-2).

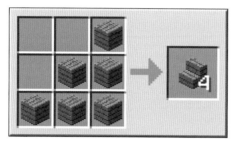

Figure 6-2: Building stairs with 6 items of the same type.

Storing More Clay in Your Inventory with Clay Block

Clay, found largely in shallow water, is easily mined with shovels. Clay balls can be crafted into a block, to allow for greater inventory storage (the clay balls can be retrieved again by breaking the clay block, and then be smelted into bricks). Storing one clay block takes up much less inventory space than 4 clay balls!

Clay blocks are rarely used as is, but are often baked in a furnace to make blast-resistant hardened clay. (See Chapter 7 for more details.) To craft clay, place 4 clay balls into a square configuration (see Figure 6-3).

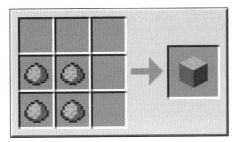

Figure 6-3: Constructing a clay block with clay balls.

Cooking Bricks

Bricks have fire immunity (as does cobblestone), making them an ideal block to build in certain situations, such as making a fireplace. Bricks are made by placing a clay ball into a furnace (see Figure 6-4).

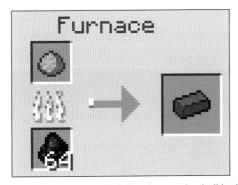

Figure 6-4: To create bricks, place a clay ball in the furnace.

Bricks can be crafted into a block, slab, or staircase.

Building with Stone Bricks

Stone brick is as blast resistant as cobblestone or brick. It's a common block that's used in strongholds. Stone brick comes in four types:

- Stone brick (by itself)
- Mossy stone brick
- Chiseled stone brick
- Cracked stone brick

Each type of stone brick has similar properties but different textures. Any mixture of stone brick can be used to craft slabs or stairs. Stone is generally more common than clay, making stone bricks more common than bricks.

The following list explains how to craft the different types of stone brick:

- **Basic stone brick:** Place 4 stone blocks into a square (see Figure 6-5).
- **Mossy stone brick:** Place a stone brick with 1 vine.
- **Chiseled stone brick:** Place 2 stone brick slabs vertically.
- **Cracked stone brick:** Place 1 stone brick into a furnace.

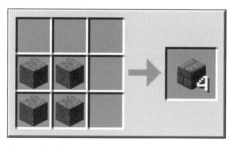

Figure 6-5: How to create a basic stone brick.

Protecting Yourself with Nether Bricks

Nether bricks are both fire resistant and blast resistant. When you build in the Nether, nether bricks make excellent shelters because they resist ghast fireballs. Nether brick blocks are formed from individual nether brick items. (Having identical names can be confusing.) The nether brick item, which looks like an individual brick, is made by placing netherrack, which is found throughout the Nether, into a furnace (similar to the instructions in Chapter 3 for mining ore).

After you obtain the nether brick items, place 4 into a square shape to create 1 nether brick block (often referred to as a nether brick). Nether brick (blocks) can further be crafted into fences, slabs, or stairs. (See Chapter 3 to find out about nether brick fences.) Figure 6-6 shows you how to make a nether brick block.

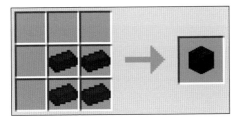

Figure 6-6: Crafting a nether brick block.

Siding with Sandstone

Sandstone is another fan-favorite texture block because of its light color. Unaffected by gravity, it remains wherever you place it, without a supporting stone. However, sandstone has much less blast resistance than wood. To overcome this problem, you can craft sandstone into slabs, giving it more of the properties of stone, including a higher blast-resistance level. Sandstone comes in these three forms:

✓ Block

✓ Smooth

✓ Chiseled

Any of these types of sandstone can be further crafted into sandstone slabs or stairs.

Red sandstone can be crafted the same way using red sandstone instead of traditional sandstone. Similarly, it can be made into blocks, smooth and chiseled sandstone, as well as slabs and stairs. Red sandstone is common in the Mesa biome. Chiseled sandstone has a creeper face on it while chiseled red sandstone has a wither depiction.

Here's how to craft the different types of sandstone:

✓ **Sandstone block:** Place 4 sand into a square configuration (see Figure 6-7).

✓ **Smooth sandstone:** Place 4 sandstone blocks into a square configuration to yield 4 blocks.

✓ **Chiseled sandstone:** Place 1 sandstone slab vertically on top of another one.

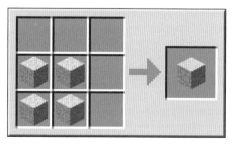

Figure 6-7: Crafting a block of sandstone with 4 pieces of sand.

Decorating with Quartz

The block of quartz, sometimes called nether quartz, is a fan favorite. Like stone bricks, quartz comes in different forms:

- ✔ Block
- ✔ Chiseled
- ✔ Pillar

You can use quartz blocks to make slabs and stairs. However, quartz recipes aren't reversible, so after the decorative quartz is crafted, it cannot be undone.

Here's how to craft the different types of quartz block:

- ✔ **Basic quartz block:** Place 4 nether quartz into a square shape (see Figure 6-8).

- ✔ **Chiseled quartz:** Place 2 quartz slabs on a vertical column.

- ✔ **Pillar quartz:** Place 2 blocks of quartz in a vertical column, yielding 2 pillars.

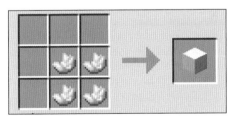

Figure 6-8: Creating a block of quartz with 4 nether quartz.

You obtain nether quartz by placing nether quartz ore into a furnace. Nether quartz is a key ingredient in daylight sensors and redstone comparator (see Chapter 5).

Navigating with Moss Stone

Moss stone is a variation of cobblestone. When placed, the stone orients so in its upper-left corner is an often hard-to-locate letter *L* pointing northeastward, making this stone (along with cobblestone and netherrack) handy for navigation.

The block, with its beautiful green-and-stone texture, is used primarily for building, especially in the Jungle and Mega Taiga biomes. To craft moss stone, place 1 cobblestone and 1 vine anywhere in the crafting grid (see Figure 6-9).

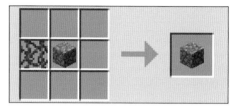

Figure 6-9: Building moss stone with cobblestone and vine.

Growing with Coarse Dirt

Coarse dirt, previously known as grassless dirt, has all the properties of dirt except that it cannot grow grass — ever. Therefore, coarse dirt can be used to create farmland using a hoe. It can also be used to create dirt structures (including walkways). However, dirt has a very low blast resistance, so it doesn't make a suitable long-term shelter.

Coarse dirt occurs naturally in the Mega Taiga, Mesa, and Savanna biomes but can be crafted as well. To craft coarse dirt, place 2 dirt and 2 gravel in a checkered square shape (see Figure 6-10).

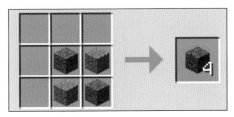

Figure 6-10: Making course dirt with dirt and gravel.

Protecting Yourself from Flames with Diorite

The igneous rock known as *diorite* is nonflammable and has a medium blast resistance similar to other stones (Level 30). An ingredient in crafting granite and andesite, it's used like any type of stone for building and can be crafted into stone slabs.

Diorite comes in two forms: (plain) diorite and polished diorite. Both have a common mixed-gray stone appearance. You craft diorite from 2 cobblestone and 2 nether quartz in a checkered square pattern (see Figure 6-11). Polished diorite is crafted from 4 diorite in a square shape and yields 4 polished diorite blocks.

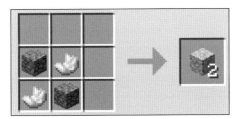

Figure 6-11: Making diorite with cobblestone and nether quartz.

Mining Granite

The multicolored brown stone known as granite also comes in both regular and polished forms. To craft, place 1 diorite and 1 nether quartz anywhere in the crafting grid (see Figure 6-12).

For polished granite, place 4 granites in a square shape to yield 4 polished blocks.

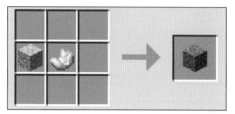

Figure 6-12: Making granite with diorite and nether quartz.

Granite requires an extra unit of nether quartz compared to diorite.

Decorating with Andesite

Like diorite and granite, the igneous rock known as andesite has stone properties and can be crafted into a traditional or polished version. It's usually found in the Extreme Hills biome, but can also be found commonly everywhere.

To craft, place a diorite and a cobblestone anywhere in the crafting grid. (It's a shapeless recipe — see Figure 6-13). To make a polished version, place 4 andesite into a square shape to yield 4 polished blocks.

Figure 6-13: Making andesite with diorite and cobblestone.

Andesite requires an extra unit of cobblestone compared to diorite.

Building from Ocean Monuments with Prismarine

The ocean monuments from the Release 1.8 update introduce 4 new blocks (prismarine, prismarine bricks, dark prismarine, and sea lantern), 2 new mobs (guardians and elder guardians), and 2 new items (prismarine shards, prismarine crystals). You can use these items to craft 3 of the 4 new blocks.

Mining prismarine shards and prismarine crystals

You obtain prismarine shards and crystals by killing guardians and elder guardians. The crystals are rarer than shards because the crystal drops only if raw fish doesn't drop, but you can also obtain the crystals by breaking sea lanterns.

You can farm prismarine shards and crystals by farming guardians, similarly to farming witches (before Version 1.7) or slimes, because they spawn only in ocean monuments. (Witches before Release 1.7 spawned only in witch huts, and slimes spawned only in the Swamp biome and slime chunks, making all three spawn only in limited spaces).

Creating prismarine

Prismarine is one of the two solid blocks that has an animation. The appearance of prismarine is coral-ish because rocks are pressed into it. The color of those rocks is aquamarine. The animated parts are the cracks between the rocks — those cracks turn from blue to green to purple.

You can find prismarine blocks in ocean monuments but you can also craft a block by placing 4 prismarine shards into a 2-by-2 square (see Figure 6-14).

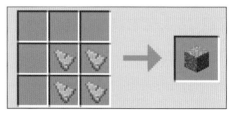

Figure 6-14: Creating prismarine with 4 prismarine shards.

Crafting prismarine bricks

Prismarine bricks are inside ocean monuments. They're paired with normal prismarine inside the monument, but they have just a slightly different texture. Prismarine bricks use the same color of prismarine and have cracks, but those cracks don't change color. The texture is a distorted green stone brick. The way to craft this beautiful block is to fill all nine spaces in the crafting grid with prismarine shards (see Figure 6-15).

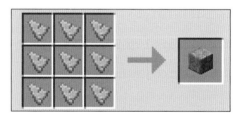

Figure 6-15: Crafting prismarine bricks with prismarine shards.

Making dark prismarine

Ah, dark prismarine — the only block we look for inside ocean monuments. Why, you ask? Because of the treasure it holds, of course. We're not visiting an ocean monument to claim the monument or collect the blocks. (Never mind. We are in the monument to collect the blocks. Have you seen how *nice* they look?)

Of course, after you take dark prismarine blocks from an ocean monument, you can also take the treasure — eight glorious gold blocks, sealed behind the dark cyan cubes that make up the dark prismarine block.

In addition to taking dark prismarine blocks as you take the prize of an ocean monument, you can also craft these blocks yourself. Place 8 prismarine shards on the outer slots of the crafting grid, and then place one ink sac in the middle (see Figure 6-16).

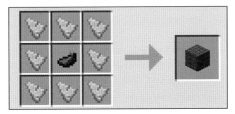

Figure 6-16: Making dark prismarine with prismarine shards.

Lighting up the sea with sea lanterns

Glorious sea lanterns bring a new light block into Minecraft — the first solid block to be animated in the game. You can just see the radiance produced by this block. It's as though a little circle is expanding inside of it. Wait — that's the animation! On the edges of this block lies an aquamarine casing, with a light aquamarine inside.

Sea lanterns, like jack-o'-lanterns and glowstone, have a light level of 15. To craft a sea lantern, you need 5 prismarine crystals (see "Mining Prismarine Shards and Prismarine Crystals" earlier in this chapter) and 4 prismarine shards. Place the 4 shards in the four corners, and place the crystals in the remaining five slots (see Figure 6-17).

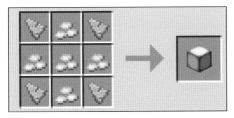

Figure 6-17: Making a sea lantern with prismarine crystals and 4 prismarine shards.

Working with Sponges

Sponges were given not only a new texture but also an old property: They can now soak up water. But wait — there's more: You can now obtain sponges in Survival mode. When a sponge is soaked in water, it's called — you guessed it — a wet sponge.

You can find wet sponges only in Survival mode, but don't worry: You can place wet sponges into a furnace to dry them and make them sponge-like again (see Figure 6-18). You can find wet sponges in certain ocean monuments: They'll be in one room, and that room will be full of wet sponges.

The new sponge texture is pure yellow with lots of *little* holes, and the wet texture in the center is a lot darker (though only slightly darker on the edges). After the wet sponge starts cooking, you can replace the fuel with an empty bucket to create a water bucket.

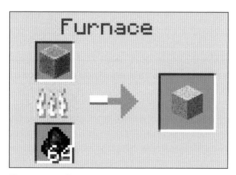

Figure 6-18: Smelting the sponge.

7

Creating and Applying Dyes

In This Chapter

- Crafting dyes
- Applying dye to wool, sheep, glass, and more
- Uncovering hidden uses for dyes

Dyes are largely decorative in Minecraft, allowing players to enhance their creations and add visual appeal. For example, you can dye wool, carpets, and glass.

But dyes can also be quite functional. A common use of dyes is in redstone wiring: Many players use dyed wool to trace their circuit lines as they create more complex mechanisms.

This chapter explains how to make the 16 different dyes and how to apply them to different items.

Creating the 16 Dyes

Minecraft has a dye for every color in the rainbow. (You can even use dyed blocks to build rainbows.) In the following sections, you find recipes for each dye.

Starting with bonemeal

Bonemeal is the color white in Minecraft. Because wool is commonly white, bonemeal is usually used as a dye ingredient in other dyes (such as lime green or pink).

To craft bonemeal, place a bone (acquired from a killed skeleton) anywhere on the crafting grid, yielding 3 bonemeal, as shown in Figure 7-1.

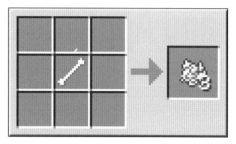

Figure 7-1: Making bonemeal.

Going gloomy (or industrial) with light gray dye

Light gray dye, which is used only as a color, can be crafted in multiple ways, such as using one of three flowers that grow randomly. Azure bluet, oxeye daisy, and white tulip all produce light gray dye when a single flower is placed anywhere in the crafting grid (see Figure 7-2). Another way is to place 2 bone-meal and 1 ink sac (from killing squids) in the grid, yielding 3 dyes. Finally, gray dye can be crafted with bonemeal to pro-duce 2 light gray dyes.

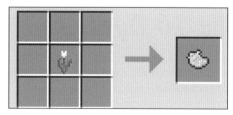

Figure 7-2: Making light gray dye with a flower.

Getting gloomier with gray dye

Gray dye is considered a secondary color in Minecraft. Though gray sheep naturally occur for gathering gray wool, gray dye can be crafted only by mixing 1 ink sac and 1 bone-meal, yielding 2 gray dyes (see Figure 7-3).

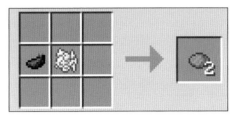

Figure 7-3: Making gray dye with an ink sac and bonemeal.

Mixing up black with ink sacs

Sheep can naturally be black, and an ink sac can be used as black dye (without crafting or smelting it in a furnace). Ink sacs are gathered from killing squids. The ink sac is a common ingredient in dyes.

Ink sacs don't exist in Survival mode in the Pocket Edition (PE) version, making both black and gray unavailable. However, you can find ink sacs in Creative mode.

Popping out rose red

Red, as its name implies, is obtained by crafting a poppy, red rose bush, or red tulip similar to the flower recipe in light gray dye. Simply place one of those flowers into a crafting grid to yield 2 red dye (see Figure 7-4).

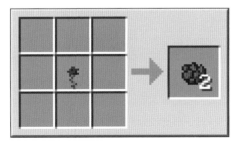

Figure 7-4: To craft rose red dye, place either a poppy, red rose bush, or red tulip on the crafting table.

In the PE version, red is crafted in the same way, because these flowers have been added in the latest update. (In earlier versions of Minecraft PE, you made red dye from beetroot.) Alternatively, the PE version enables you to make red dye by placing a red mushroom into a furnace (see Figure 7-5). Red, a primary color, is a common ingredient in making secondary colors.

Figure 7-5: Crafting red by placing a red mushroom in a furnace.

Prettying with pink

You can mix together pink dye in one of two ways:

- Use 1 pink tulip or 1 peony (flowers) placed anywhere in the crafting grid. Doing so yields 2 pink dye if created with peony, or 1 pink dye if created with a pink tulip (see Figure 7-6).

- Place 1 red dye and 1 bonemeal into the grid. It yields 2 pink dyes (see Figure 7-7).

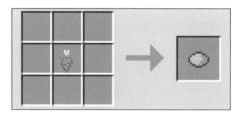

Figure 7-6: Making pink dye with a pink tulip.

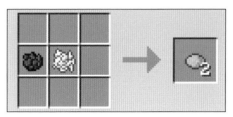

Figure 7-7: Making pink dye by placing red dye and bonemeal in the crafting grid.

Making dandelion yellow dye

The primary color dandelion yellow dye is crafted by placing a dandelion or sunflower into the crafting grid, yielding 2 dyes (see Figure 7-8).

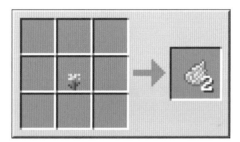

Figure 7-8: Creating yellow dye with a dandelion or sunflower.

Crafting orange dye

You can create orange dye by crafting orange tulips (see Figure 7-9) or by combining a rose red dye with dandelion yellow dye, yielding 2 orange (see Figure 7-10).

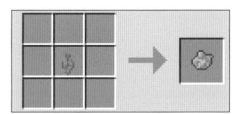

Figure 7-9: Using orange tulips to make orange dye.

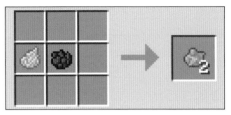

Figure 7-10: Using red dye and dandelion yellow dye to make orange dye.

Making cactus green dye

Green is considered a primary color in Minecraft and is therefore a crafting ingredient in other dyes. You craft green by smelting cactus in a furnace (see Figure 7-11).

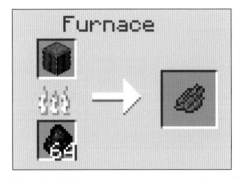

Figure 7-11: You make cactus green dye by smelting cactus in a furnace.

Mixing lime dye

Lime, a secondary color, is crafted by placing cactus green dye and bonemeal anywhere in the crafting grid, yielding two lime dyes (see Figure 7-12).

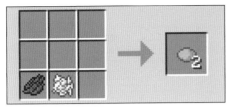

Figure 7-12: Making lime dye by placing cactus green and bonemeal on the crafting grid.

Mining blue lapis lazuli

As we describe in Chapter 3, lapis lazuli is obtained by mining. When you mine lapis lazuli with a stone pickaxe (or better), you get 4–8 pieces for your inventory. You can use lapis lazuli immediately as dye or craft lapis lazuli into various items, including a block for building or decorating. Although lapis lazuli doesn't need to be smelted or crafted as a dye, you can use it in other dye recipes.

Making light blue dye

Light blue can be created by crafting a blue orchid anywhere in the crafting grid (see Figure 7-13) or by combining lapis lazuli with bonemeal, yielding 2 light blue dyes (see Figure 7-14).

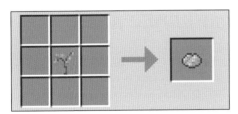

Figure 7-13: Making light blue dye by placing a blue orchid on the crafting table.

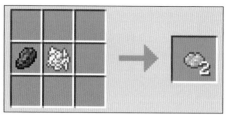

Figure 7-14: Making light blue dye by combining lapis lazuli with bonemeal.

Aquafying things with cyan

Cyan, a blend of green and blue, is a secondary color that's commonly used to achieve an aquatic look. To craft, place 1 cactus green and 1 lapis lazuli anywhere in the grid to yield two cyan dyes (see Figure 7-15).

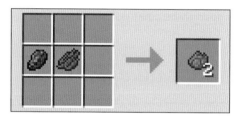

Figure 7-15: Making cyan dye by placing 1 cactus green and 1 lapis lazuli on the crafting table.

Preparing purple dye

Purple, a secondary color, is created by placing 1 lapis lazuli and 1 rose red anywhere in the crafting grid to yield 2 purple dyes (see Figure 7-16). Purple is commonly used to create a royal effect when applied to decorative blocks. You can also use purple dye to create magenta dye.

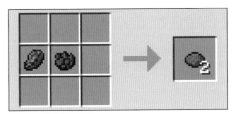

Figure 7-16: Making purple dye by placing lapis lazuli and rose red dyes on the crafting table.

Coloring with magenta

Magenta can be crafted from allium (yielding 1 dye) or a lilac (yielding 2 dye) placed anywhere in the crafting grid (see Figure 7-17) or by placing 1 purple and 1 pink dye anywhere in the crafting grid, yielding 2 dyes (see Figure 7-18).

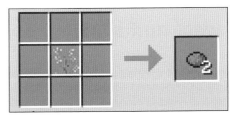

Figure 7-17: Making magenta dye with lilac.

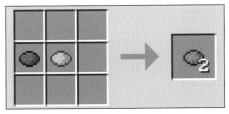

Figure 7-18: Making magenta dye with purple and pink dyes.

Because purple can be broken into lapis lazuli and rose red and pink can be broken into rose red and bonemeal, placing those 4 ingredients together (2 rose red, 1 bonemeal, 1 lapis lazuli) also produces magenta, without having to craft the intermediate ingredients of purple and pink.

Finding brown dye

Similar to black and blue, brown isn't crafted. You just need to find cocoa beans in the jungle biome. Cocoa beans can also be farmed, as explained in Chapter 3.

Though also a food item, cocoa beans are recognized as a dye when you apply them.

Applying Dye to Items

You can apply any dye to wool, sheep, the collar of tame wolves, firework stars, leather armor, glass, and clay. When you want to dye an item, you can choose any color you like for the dye part of the recipe. The following sections explain how to dye all these different items.

Dyeing wool and sheep

Wool can be dyed in two ways. The first is to place any dye and a wool block on the crafting grid, yielding a block of dyed wool (see Figure 7-19). Second, sheep can be directly dyed by holding the dye and right-clicking on the sheep. This action permanently dyes the sheep, allowing it to be sheared multiple times and always yielding the same color (see Figure 7-20).

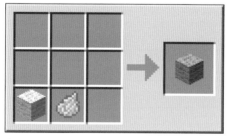

Figure 7-19: Making dyed wool by placing any dye and a wool block on the crafting table.

Figure 7-20: Making dyed wool by simply holding the dye and right-clicking on the sheep.

Also, when two sheep mate, the offspring roughly follows the laws of genetics, allowing for the baby to be the color of one parent or a secondary color created by blending the parents' color (for you parents, effectively teaching your children biology!). Many players enjoy watching this interaction on their sheep farms.

In addition to the decorative uses of dyed wool, many players color-code their mines and redstone circuits using dyed wool.

Sheep naturally come in white, gray, light gray, black, brown, and (rarely) pink. Regardless of the sheep's color, when a new dye in placed on the sheep or wool, it immediately takes that color. Therefore, sheep don't need to be dyed bonemeal white before being dyed to a new color, nor does dyeing a white sheep to become rose red yield a pink sheep. (It would yield a rose red sheep.)

Crafting and dyeing carpets

A carpet is a decorative block but is helpful when building and farming. It can be used for a more effective table than pressure plates, and because the Pocket Edition (PE) has no pressure plates yet, Pocket Edition users use brown carpet.

Mobs such as zombies don't count carpets as a block they can walk on. So a carpet is a great way to prevent mobs from entering a home or other structure if you don't have a door. Simply dig a hole 3 blocks down where the entrance to your structure is, placing a sign on the first block from the top in the hole and then place carpet on top of the sign. To you it looks and acts like a normal entrance, but to a mob, they won't enter!

For farming, you can put wool on fence posts, which is helpful to get in and out of your farm easily: Jump onto the carpet, and then walk on top of the fence. Cows and sheep and other animals don't think they can jump on the carpet, so they stay in their pens.

Towering, or the process of reaching new altitudes in Minecraft, is simple with carpets: You can put a carpet on top of a carpet and when you come down from a higher altitude, simply break the carpet that's on the ground. All the rest of the carpets then break and fall down. Interestingly, carpet has no texture, because it uses the wool texture.

To craft a carpet, place 2 pieces of wool in a horizontal row, yielding three carpets (see Figure 7-21). To dye the carpet, you must first dye the wool that the carpet is made from.

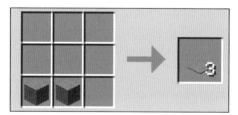

Figure 7-21: Making a carpet with wool.

Changing the color of wolf collars

Tamed wolves (often called *dogs*) have red collars. You can change the color by right-clicking on the tamed wolf while holding the dye. You can then organize groups of tamed wolves or separate your pack from another player's pack in a multiplayer game.

Making stained glass with dyed glass panes

Glass can be stained any of the 16 dye colors and is commonly used as a decorative block. Glass panes cannot be dyed after they're crafted, and you can't change the color of glass after you dye it.

To create stained glass, you dye the glass blocks, turn those blocks into panes, and the panes retain the color of the glass blocks. Players can then create stained-glass window pane designs by stacking the newly created panes in the desired pattern.

Stained glass functions like glass, with one exception: You cannot place a torch on top of stained glass. To craft, place dye in the center square with 8 surrounding blocks of glass, yielding 8 dyed glass blocks (see Figure 7-22).

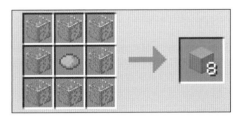

Figure 7-22: To stain glass, use any color dye with 8 blocks of glass.

Stained clay

Like glass blocks, clay can be dyed only once. Clay is less vibrant in color, but is a stronger building block than wool because of its fire and blast resistance. Clay blocks are smelted to become hardened before they can be dyed, so a more accurate term is *stained hardened clay*.

To craft stained clay, place the dye in the center square surrounded by 8 hardened clay, yielding 8 stained hardened clay blocks (see Figure 7-23).

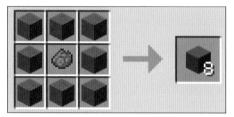

Figure 7-23: Crafting stained clay with dye and hardened clay.

Dyed leather armor

Leather itself cannot be dyed, but you can dye leather armor. To do so, place a piece of armor (boots and helmet, for example) into the crafting grid with a dye (see Figure 7-24).

If you change your mind about your armor color, you can re-dye it, but the resulting color blends the current color with the new color. Leather armor can therefore be a combination of shades, depending on how many times it has been dyed (over 12 million combinations). As in real life, the armor color can never become darker without using a darker dye color. To return leather armor to its natural color, you need to place it in a cauldron (see Chapter 8 to learn how to use and find a cauldron).

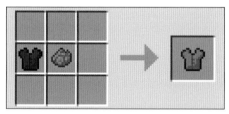

Figure 7-24: Dyeing leather with a piece of armor and your dye of choice.

8

Enchantment and Brewing Recipes

In This Chapter

▶ Creating enchantment and brewing tools

▶ Learning to enchant

▶ Mastering brewing

*O*ur fellow Minecraft wizards: The most advanced part of Minecraft is its enchantments and brewing potions. You have to create the enchantment table and brewing stand, and you need to have earned enough Experience points (which varies depending on which enchantment or potion you want to use) to use them. Ingredients are often rare, but the rewards are tremendous. This chapter walks you through the steps to become a master potion maker.

Enchantment and brewing are among the most rewarding parts of Minecraft, but the rewards come later in the gameplay. Both enchanting and brewing require practice and patience, so that you maximize the result you want with the resources you have at hand.

Building an Enchantment Table

For many players, the first experience in the magical side of Minecraft is via the enchantment table. To craft an enchantment table, you need 4 obsidian, 2 diamond, and a book (see Figure 8-1).

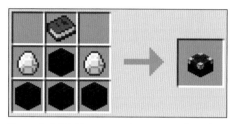

Figure 8-1: Making an enchantment table with obsidian, diamond, and a book.

Because both obsidian and diamonds are rare, you cannot create an enchantment table until later in the gameplay.

Picking an Enchantment, Any Enchantment

The availability of enchantments ranges from low to high and requires Experience points and bookshelves. To reach the highest levels of enchantment, 15 bookshelves need to surround your enchantment table. (However, the bookshelves don't have to be connected.)

To achieve a lower enchantment, you should place a block, such as a piece of carpet or a torch, between the enchantment table and a bookcase. Unfortunately, you don't fully control which enchantment is available.

After constructing an enchantment table, here's how to enchant a tool or armor:

1. **Open up your enchanting screen by right-clicking the enchantment table.**

   The enchanting screen will show, with a place where you can place items, and 3 buttons.

2. **Select the tool or armor or other item (like a book) to be enchanted.**

   Hoes, shears, and horse armor cannot be enchanted on a table.

3. **Power the enchantment table with lapis lazuli.**

   In the latest version of Minecraft, in order to enchant things, your enchantment table must be powered with lapis lazuli. You do so by placing lapis lazuli in the second block on the enchantment table (see Figure 8-2). Place the same number of lapis lazuli as you have numbers on the right.

   Then you're given three options, displaying only the Experience points required for the spell, and, by moving your mouse over the option, one of the enchantments that you are guaranteed to get, with a one, two, or three as your price. You aren't given any indication if you will gain any other enchantments for the item you are enchanting however.

4. **Choose one of the three options randomly.**

   The options are labeled using a special language (with characters called "runes") but even when ciphered, the combination of runes doesn't disclose the enchantment (see Figure 8-2). The higher the level option, the higher level enchantment you will receive. To know what the item was enchanted with, mouse over the item in your inventory and the enchantment will appear under the item name.

   To get around the problem of not knowing what an item will be enchanted with, many players choose to enchant a book, revealing the enchantment, and then use the book on an anvil to apply a specific enchantment to the desired item. For a list of enchantments, see Table 8-1.

The one, two, and three are your cost. Choosing one means you will have to pay one experience point, and one lapis lazuli. Paying three means you will have to pay three experience points and three lapis lazuli.

Figure 8-2: The enchantment GUI in version 1.8.

Table 8-1   Enchantments

Enchantment	Effect	Item
Protection	Reduces damage	Armor
Fire protection	Reduces fire damage	Armor
Feather falling	Reduces fall damage	Boots
Blast protection	Reduces explosion damage	Armor
Thorns	Damages attacker	Armor (helmet, boots, leggings only on anvil)
Projectile protection	Reduces projectile damage	Armor
Aqua infinity	Increases underwater mining speed	Helmet
Respiration	Increases underwater breathing	Helmet
Depth strider	Increases underwater movement	Boots
Looting	Increases mob drops	Sword
Knockback	Increases the range that a mob is thrown when hit	Sword

Enchantment	Effect	Item
Fire aspect	Sets items on fire	Sword
Bane of anthropods	Increase damage to spiders, silverfish, and endermites	Sword and ax (ax only on anvil)
Sharpness	Increases damage	Sword and ax (ax only on anvil)
Smite	Increases damage to skeletons, zombies, and withers	Sword and ax (ax only on anvil)
Fortune	Increases block drops	Sword, shovel, ax
Silk touch	Mined blocks drop themselves	Pickaxe, shovel, ax, and shears (shears on anvil)
Efficiency	Increases mining speed	Pickaxe, shovel, ax, and shears (shears on anvil)
Lure	Increases rate of fish biting	Fishing pole
Luck of the sea	Decreases odds of junk when fishing	Fishing pole
Infinity	Shooting uses up no arrows	Bow
Punch	Increases knockback	Bow
Flame	Sets arrows on fire	Bow
Power	Increases damage	Bow
Unbreaking	Increases durability	Armor, sword, bow, fishing pole, axe, shovel, and pickaxe; using an anvil — shears, flint and steel, carrot on a stick, and hoe

Making Brewing Tools

If you want to survive in the game, you'll want to eventually get into brewing. Brewing potions enables you to do anything from increasing your life, to speeding up your step, or to even seeing in the dark. In this section we'll show you some of the really cool things you can do to improve your game using potions. We start by showing you the tools you need to start brewing.

Making glass bottles

Essential to brewing potions, glass bottles provide the water for a brewing stand (see the section "Making a brewing stand," later in this chapter) and hold the resulting potion. They're easily crafted from 3 glass blocks placed in a v shape in the crafting grid, yielding 3 bottles (see Figure 8-3).

To fill a glass bottle with water, hold the bottle in your hand, and right-click on a water source, or a filled cauldron. Keep in mind that some of the cauldron will be emptied if you fill your glass bottle from the cauldron.

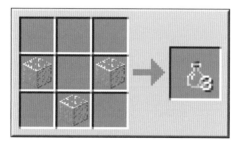

Figure 8-3: To make glass bottles, place 3 glass in a V shape.

Brewing in cauldrons

A *cauldron* has two main functions:

- **Hold water in the Nether.** Buckets of water evaporate.
- **Wash the dye from leather armor.** To wash dye from your leather armor, hold the armor in your hand, and right-click the cauldron.

You craft a cauldron by placing 7 iron ingots in a U shape on the crafting grid (see Figure 8-4). Because a cauldron requires more iron to craft than a bucket, players often make the cauldron much later in the game.

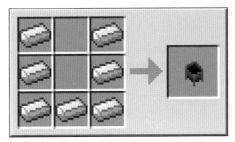

Figure 8-4: Making a cauldron with iron ingots.

Making a brewing stand

A *brewing stand* is used to make potions. One of its ingredients, a blaze rod, is obtained in the Nether. Similar to an enchantment table, a brewing stand has its own GUI, featuring a slot in the top for a primary ingredient and three slots in the bottom for water bottles, which will ultimately hold the complete potion. To craft a brewing stand, place 3 cobblestone in the bottom horizontal row with a blaze rod in the middle slot (see Figure 8-5).

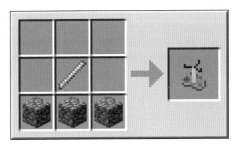

Figure 8-5: Making a brewing stand with cobblestone and a blaze rod.

Crafting Brewing Ingredients

Most of the items in brewing require crafting. In the section, "Making Glass Bottles" earlier in this chapter, we discuss making water bottles and having a source of water available for brewing (often, a bucket that was also crafted). This section, on the other hand, looks at the crafted ingredients used in brewing potions.

Making blaze powder

Blaze powder is used in brewing mundane and strength potions. You craft *blaze powder* by simply placing a blaze rod into the crafting grid, yielding 2 blaze powder (see Figure 8-6). This ingredient, found in a fire charge (see Chapter 4), is commonly used in brewing. You obtain blaze powder from a blaze (found in the Nether).

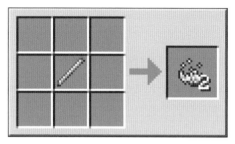

Figure 8-6: Making blaze powder with a blaze rod.

Making magma cream

Magma cream is used largely to brew fire-resistance potions. You craft it by placing blaze powder and a slimeball anywhere in the crafting grid (see Figure 8-7).

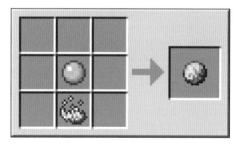

Figure 8-7: Magna cream is created with blaze powder and a slimeball.

Making the eye of ender

Eye of ender, used in ender chests, is crucial in helping you reach the End. Eye of ender isn't used in brewing, but is crafted from blaze powder — making this recipe available only after you have defeated a blaze in the Nether and crafted powder from blaze rods. To craft an eye of ender, place an ender pearl and blaze powder anywhere in the crafting grid (see Figure 8-8).

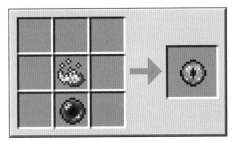

Figure 8-8: Making eye of ender with an ender pearl and blaze powder.

Brewing fermented spider eye

Fermented spider eye, which is one of the most powerful potion ingredients, is regularly made into a splash potion to be used as a weapon. You use fermented spider eye to brew potions of weakness, invisibility, slowness, and harming; you craft fermented spider eye by placing a brown mushroom, a sugar, and a spider eye anywhere in the crafting grid (see Figure 8-9).

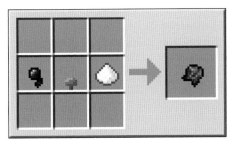

Figure 8-9: Making fermented spider eye with brown mushroom, sugar, and spider eye.

Healing with glistening melon

Glistening melon is one of the easier brewing ingredients to obtain; it's used in healing potions. You craft it from a slice of melon placed in the center slot and surrounded by 8 gold nuggets. Melon slices are easily farmed, and a single gold ingot produces 9 gold nuggets (1 more than is needed for this recipe). See Figure 8-10 for an example.

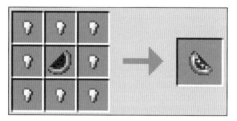

Figure 8-10: Making glistening melon with a melon slice and gold nuggets.

Golden apples and golden carrots are foods with tremendous Health, Hunger, and Saturation points. However, glistening melon, despite being gold and made of a food item, isn't a food and cannot be eaten.

Understanding Brewing

Each brewing potion begins with a water bottle placed in a lower slot on the brewing stand. You can more efficiently place 3 bottles filled with water in the brewing stand, because it requires no additional ingredients (beyond the 2 extra water bottles) and yields 3 completed potions.

The next step is to place a primary ingredient into the top of the stand. The vast majority of potions are derived from nether wart, a plant found and grown in the Nether, yielding an awkward potion (see Figure 8-11). Consequently, you need to gather a stock of nether wart from the Nether (either grown, or found in chests and staircases within Nether fortresses, or on soul sand on console editions) before becoming a brewing master. The other major potion is one of weakness, which is brewed from a fermented spider eye (see Figure 8-12).

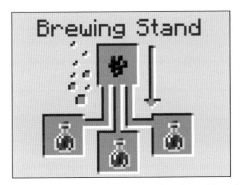

Figure 8-11: Making an awkward potion with nether wart.

Figure 8-12: Making a weakness potion with a fermented spider eye.

Brewing requires multiple steps, a stockpile of ingredients (including a water source), and time, because each brewing step takes 20 seconds. Many players ensure that they have the ability to complete the process before starting it.

Making positive potions

All positive potions listed in this section require a bottle of awkward potion (or more efficiently, 3 bottles of awkward potion) to be placed into the bottom of the brewing stand. Then you place the ingredient in the top of the brewing stand to produce the desired potion — see Table 8-2.

Table 8-2	Positive Potions	
Name	*Ingredient*	*Effect*
Fire resistance	Magma cream	Create immunity from fire, including lava and blaze, for example.
Healing	Glistening melon	Restore 2 hearts on the Health bar.
Leaping	Rabbit's foot (dropped by rabbits)	You can jump half a block higher.
Night vision	Golden carrot	You can see as though you're in full light.
Regeneration	Ghast tear (dropped by ghasts when they are killed)	Add health hearts over time.
Strength (see Figure 8-13)	Blaze powder	Add damage to all melee attacks.
Swiftness	Sugar	Increase speed and jumping length.
Water breathing	Pufferfish (caught by fishing)	You can swim underwater without affecting the oxygen level.

Figure 8-13: The strength positive brewing recipe.

Concocting negative potions

Negative potions produce undesirable effects. Similar to positive potions, most negative potions also begin with an awkward potion and adding ingredients. The exception is a potion of weakness, which can be brewed from glowstone or redstone in the first brewing step. Table 8-3 lists the brewing ingredients and their effects.

Table 8-3	Negative Potions	
Potion	*Ingredient*	*Effect*
Poison	Spider eye	Player is poisoned, which reduces Health points half a heart at a time.
Weakness	Fermented spider eye	Melee attacks are reduced.
Harming	Fermented spider eye, added to poison or healing potion	Reduces 3 hearts (6 Health points).
Slowness (see Figure 8-14)	Fermented spider eye, added to fire, leaping, or swiftness potion	You can move only as fast as a crouch.

Figure 8-14: Create the negative potion of slowness with fermented spider eye and a fire, leaping, or swiftness potion.

Negative potions are created to be used against mobs because they produce a negative effect. Therefore, negative potions must be turned into splash potions in order to kill mobs by adding gunpowder to the top of the brewing stand, allowing the completed potion to be thrown.

Brewing advanced potions

Brewing redstone into a potion generally extends the length of time that the effect lasts; adding glowstone increases the potion strength to the next level (from Tier I to Tier II). This works for both positive and negative potions. To brew one of these potions, place an existing positive or negative potion (such as potion of fire resistance) on the brewing stand, and add redstone or glowstone dust.

When you use redstone and glowstone together, they cancel each other out.

Making the potion of invisibility

The unique potion of invisibility combines the ingredients of positive and negative potions, which is why we don't cover it in the tables earlier in this chapter. To create a potion of invisibility, place a potion of night vision (a positive potion) to the bottom of the brewing stand and add a fermented spider eye (a negative ingredient) to the top (see Figure 8-15).

Figure 8-15: To make the invisibility potion, add a potion of night vision and a fermented spider eye to the brewing stand.

9
Ten Essential Minecraft Ingredients

In This Chapter

▸ Exploring ten essential ingredients

▸ Obtaining and maximizing these ingredients

*W*ith more than 200 Minecraft recipes, including smelting and brewing recipes, a handful of ingredients are common across several types of recipes. This chapter helps you examine the ten essential ingredients that you need to acquire and then put in the inventory to advance through crafting things in Minecraft.

Building the Basics with Wood

Wood is the basic ingredient that interlinks all craftable items in Minecraft. You cannot finish the game, or even advance in it, without wood. The first thing a player does in Minecraft is punch (or harvest by hitting things like trees with the item in your hand) wood, often using it to create survival items for the first night — a sword, bed, shelter, and crafting table.

You can also obtain wood by chopping, digging, mining, slicing, or basically breaking it in any way possible. It has 6 different variations (see Figure 9-1): oak, birch, spruce, jungle, dark oak, and acacia. Each type has a different texture and is found in a different biome.

Figure 9-1: Wood has six various textures.

Wood is generally crafted into planks and then used in crafting an impressive number of items, including buttons, fences, boats, ladders, planks, torches, trapdoors, doors, signs, bowls, wooden weapons, and tools. Wood not crafted into planks is also an essential ingredient in the furnace — it can be the fuel as well as the ingredient that's smelted into charcoal (even though it would be more efficient to use planks as the fuel and just burn the wood for charcoal).

Wielding Sticks to Advance in the Game

From planks to sticks, from sticks to picks, and from picks to the very end — yes, my friend, we are talking about sticks. You obtain sticks by crafting wooden planks.

Considering that sticks are made of wood, it shows the power of wood in Minecraft. Wood is so important that we have distinguished wood and sticks as two of the ten essential ingredients.

Sticks are used in recipes for diverse products, including the examples in this list:

- ↗ **Tools:** Pickaxe, axe, shovel, and hoe
- ↗ **Redstone:** Tripwire hook and redstone torch
- ↗ **Weapons:** Sword, arrow, and bow
- ↗ **Rails:** Detector, activator, powered, and rail itself
- ↗ **All fences and ladders also require sticks**
- ↗ **Household items:** Signs and paintings

Sticks are used in a total of 21 recipes. Though sticks are crafted from any of the six types of wood, all sticks have the same texture and properties. A full stack in the inventory requires 32 wood planks.

Adding Texture with Wool

Carpets are wooly, beds are wooly, mammoths are wooly, and wool is wooly. In your Minecraft recipes, wool is the only way to go to bed and style your house. You can easily obtain wool by killing sheep, using string in a 2-by-2 square, or finding black wool in a village (found on lampposts, which are black blocks of wool with 4 torches around them). A more efficient way to get wool is to shear sheep; that action gives you 1 to 3 blocks of wool, and sheep can regrow their "coats" by eating grass and tall grass.

Wool can be dyed into 16 different colors (see Chapter 7). To dye wool, place the wool and the dye of your choosing in the crafting table. You can also find sheep with an already dyed coat or simply dye the sheep yourself (again, see Chapter 7 to learn more about dyeing). Dyed sheep remain dyed even when you shear them. When their coats grow back, they're still the color you chose for dye. Natural sheep can be brown, black, gray, light gray, the common white, and the rare pink sheep.

Wool (used in recipes for carpets, paintings, and beds) is considered an essential ingredient because of bed crafting, which is considered a significant part of your survival efforts on your first night and later. Wool can also be used in advanced redstone circuitry.

Feeding Yourself and Animals with Wheat

Though you cannot eat wheat in its raw, natural form, combined and converted into other foods, it can be quite nutritious! Wheat is obtained by the wheat crop, but it can also be uncrafted from hay bales.

By punching (hitting things by holding down your mouse button) long grass, you have a chance of getting wheat seeds, which can be planted into farmland. Wheat grows in 8 stages, growing taller and changing shape in each one. You know when wheat's fully grown because it turns from a yellow green to a darkened yellow. After it's fully grown it drops 1 wheat and 0 to 3 seeds. If destroyed and not fully grown, wheat drops only seeds.

Wheat — which can be crafted into bread, cake, cookies, and hay bales — is the most common type of farm created by Minecraft players. (Figure 9-2 shows a wheat farm.) It can be not only crafted into edible items but also used in breeding animals.

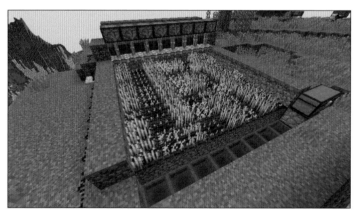

Figure 9-2: A wheat farm in Minecraft.

Building the Basics with Cobblestone

Cobblestone, with its dark texture, is an interesting block. In the past, it has changed to a lighter texture, which changed to a more detailed texture, which changed to an even lighter texture — the same texture it has now. Between the time of the more detailed texture and its current texture was a small window of time where cobblestone was removed from the game because of space limitations.

You may already know that cobblestone was the first block added to Minecraft. It's now used to create all sorts of items, including andesite (see Chapter 6), stone axe, brewing stand, cobblestone wall (big surprise), diorite, dispenser, dropper, furnace, stone hoe, lever, moss stone, stone pick, piston, stone shovel, cobblestone slab, cobblestone stairs, stonecutter (PE exclusive), and stone sword.

Shooting Items with Gunpowder

Gunpowder destroys your enemies, and gunpowder has some explosive recipes. Obtaining it is somewhat tricky because you have to defeat some hard mobs. However, after you kill them, gunpowder isn't hard to find. To get some, you need to kill a creeper or a ghast or a witch. You can also find gunpowder in dungeons.

You can use gunpowder to craft fire charges, firework rockets, firework stars, and TNT. Many players (like Thomas's younger brother) love TNT — I mean, *really* love TNT — so gunpowder is one of their favorite ingredients.

Additionally, gunpowder is the only ingredient that can brew a splash potion (see Figure 9-3). Many players prefer splash potions to positive potions, making gunpowder a fan favorite among brewing masters.

Figure 9-3: Constructing a splash potion using gunpowder.

Building Solid Tools with Iron Ingot

Iron is an important ingredient to advance you throughout the game of Minecraft — it's found everywhere. Look under your house, in a mountain, in your favorite cave, in your least favorite cave, under your porch, and pretty much everywhere underground. You can find iron in ore form, but smelting the ore makes it useful, by turning the iron ore into iron ingots.

Add some sticks and you have an iron sword, iron pickaxe, axe, shovel, or hoe. And you can craft activator rails, anvils, blocks of iron, iron boots, buckets, cauldrons, iron chest-plates, compasses, detector rails, iron doors, flint and steel, iron helmets, hoppers, iron bars, iron leggings, minecarts, nether reactor cores (PE exclusive), pistons, rails, shears, iron trapdoors, tripwire hooks, and heavy weighted pressure plates. Perhaps we should simply say that iron ingots are an ingredient in 27 recipes, making iron ingot the item with the most recipes in the desktop version of the game.

Enchanting with Gold Ingot

When you strike gold, you're probably thinking that you're rich — well, rich in rails, clocks, and apples, anyway. To obtain gold, you have to dig deep or kill pigmen. You have to smelt gold ore in a furnace to get gold ingots. You can also craft gold ingots with 9 gold nuggets or uncraft a block of gold into 9 ingots. Gold is also used to craft the 4 basic tools (pickaxe, axe, shovel, and hoe), but they can also be used to craft a sword and the 4 pieces of armor (helmet, chestplate, pair of leggings, and pair of boots).

All these gold recipes have a high enchantment rate — you get better enchantments but with low durability. Additionally, the gold pickaxe, axe, and shovel break most blocks faster than the other tools do, including diamond, but they all have a durability of 33. You can also craft a block of gold, a clock, gold nuggets, golden apples, powered rails, and a light weighted pressure plate.

Thinking Logically with Redstone

Redstone is the most powerful, and perhaps the most fun (or most mind-wrecking, depending on your standpoint) of all the stones. After you find it, its effects can be life-changing. Redstone powers all redstone contraptions and can be used to manipulate rails. Figure 9-4 shows a simple redstone contraption that has a button, and when you push the button to open a door, instead of opening it, it takes you below the door, and then back up on the other side! (See the *Minecraft For Dummies* YouTube channel for an example.)

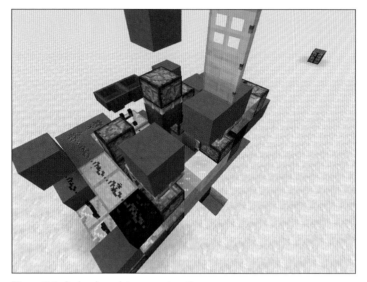

Figure 9-4: A simple redstone contraption

Without redstone, Minecraft would have no automatic farms, no automatic brewing machines, no powered pistons, no traps, no one-hit xp-farms, or (most important!) no piston doors. Redstone is used in making redstone torches, repeaters, compasses, clocks, redstone blocks, detector rails, dispensers, droppers, noteblocks, pistons, powered rails, and redstone lamps. Additionally, redstone is used to extend potions. You can also place it down where you can then use it to allow the function of other objects, but you need to power the redstone with a redstone torch or a redstone block.

Discovering Diamonds

Roses are red
Diamonds are blue
I couldn't think of anything better to say
So this part is up to you.

Imagine that you're digging deep into your favorite cave, and then you see the light blue ore. You dig into the ore and see that there are four diamonds. You barely glance at the words in the upper right corner of your screen: DIAMONDS. Your favorite cave just became that much sweeter.

But you can obtain diamonds in alternative ways: You can uncraft the block of diamond, or you can find them in a chest at a village or desert temple. (That would be your lucky day.) As with most ores (the exceptions are iron and gold), another method — smelting diamonds — is inefficient. It doesn't give you as much experience as mining it regularly, and when smelting diamonds you don't get to benefit from the fortune effect enchantment. (People can usually get diamonds when they break diamond ore with a pickaxe enchanted with the fortune enchantment — or "fortune pick" as it is nicknamed — so they can mine it and get more diamonds for it; see Figure 9-5.)

Obtaining diamond ore in Survival mode is difficult. To get diamond ore, you need to mine the ore with a pickaxe that has been enchanted with the silk touch enchantment.

Figure 9-5: A diamond mine.

Diamond is considered end game material, so don't expect to find it on your first day. Diamonds are used to craft many items, including basic tools and armor, which are your axe, hoe, pickaxe, shovel, boots, chestplate, helmet, and leggings. Diamond tools and armor are in the top tier, with the most durability, damage, speed, and damage deduction. The other items that are crafted with diamonds are block of diamond, enchantment table, jukebox, and nether reactor core (PE exclusive). Additionally, adding a diamond to the firework star recipe gives the firework star the trail effect.

Index

Notes

Notes

Notes

Notes

Notes

Notes

Notes

Notes

Notes

Notes

About the Authors

Jesse Stay, "The Social Geek," studies and learns about new business-altering paradigm shifts in technology, and shows businesses how to embrace these paradigm shifts before their competition does. He has written 8 books, helped design some of the top apps on Facebook, and has been recognized as one of the top 20 developers to follow on Twitter by Mashable next to Jack Dorsey, and top 10 entrepreneurs to follow on Twitter by Mashable and Entrepreneur magazine next to Ev Williams, Biz Stone, and Guy Kawasaki.

Jesse started as a software developer, programming computers since he was 10 years old living in Jakarta, Indonesia. An entrepreneur at heart, he discovered a desire to grow audiences and customers for the apps he built, but lacked the skills to do so. His only option was to go out and hire an expensive marketer, SEO, or social media professional to help with app growth. He decided this needed to change, and applied his software skills to a proven program for cultivating and growing large audiences that convert.

Jesse now speaks internationally; writes books; performs webinars; and coaches for individuals, businesses, and organizations looking to take their marketing to that next level using social media and other techniques. Jesse plays Minecraft with his 4 sons when he has free time.

Thomas Stay is Jesse's 12-year-old son, who eats, drinks, and breathes Minecraft. Thomas programs in Python and JavaScript, and blogs at `http://tom.staynalive.com`, where he writes about programming and software development. Thomas is a straight-A student, excels in the Utah State Chess championships, and is already enrolled in one grade ahead of his age group.

Dedication

To Rebecca (or Mom), who really put more effort into this book than any of us did. The person who truly deserves their name on the front of this book is her.

This was truly a family effort, and like the rest of our family, Mom was the one who powered it, kept it going, and even dug in and made it happen. As you're reading this book, while they are Thomas and Jesse's words, you'll catch a hint of Mom throughout. Rebecca and Mom, we couldn't have done it without you!

Authors' Acknowledgments

Thanks to the entire family for pitching in on this. Even our friends who would all place their characters in one spot so we could get a screenshot, the Rikers who would let us use their Minecraft server until we could set up our own, and Hunter who helped get us into some of this world of Minecraft.

Thanks to Joseph and JJ for pitching in a few screenshots, and to Alex and Emily and even our big sister Elizabeth for letting us use the computer and devices while we played the game to be able to write this book.

Lastly, as always thanks to all the great editors at Wiley – Amy Fandrei, Rebecca (Becky) Huehls, Jennifer Webb, and the many others that made this work! I (Jesse) have done many of these, but it always takes a good editor to bring back memories of how to do it "the right" way!

Publisher's Acknowledgments

Acquisitions Editor: Amy Fandrei

Senior Project Editor: Rebecca Huehls

Copy Editor: Becky Whitney

Technical Editor: Ryan Nelson

Editorial Assistant: Claire Johnson

Sr. Editorial Assistant: Cherie Case

Project Coordinator: Sheree Montgomery

Cover Photo: Courtesy of Jesse Stay

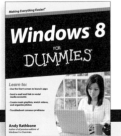

Math & Science

Algebra I For Dummies,
2nd Edition
978-0-470-55964-2

Anatomy and Physiology
For Dummies, 2nd Edition
978-0-470-92326-9

Astronomy For Dummies,
3rd Edition
978-1-118-37697-3

Biology For Dummies,
2nd Edition
978-0-470-59875-7

Chemistry For Dummies,
2nd Edition
978-1-118-00730-3

1001 Algebra II Practice
Problems For Dummies
978-1-118-44662-1

Microsoft Office

Excel 2013 For Dummies
978-1-118-51012-4

Office 2013 All-in-One
For Dummies
978-1-118-51636-2

PowerPoint 2013 For Dummies
978-1-118-50253-2

Word 2013 For Dummies
978-1-118-49123-2

Music

Blues Harmonica For Dummies
978-1-118-25269-7

Guitar For Dummies, 3rd Edition
978-1-118-11554-1

iPod & iTunes For Dummies,
10th Edition
978-1-118-50864-0

Programming

Beginning Programming with C
For Dummies
978-1-118-73763-7

Excel VBA Programming
For Dummies, 3rd Edition
978-1-118-49037-2

Java For Dummies, 6th Edition
978-1-118-40780-6

Religion & Inspiration

The Bible For Dummies
978-0-7645-5296-0

Buddhism For Dummies,
2nd Edition
978-1-118-02379-2

Catholicism For Dummies,
2nd Edition
978-1-118-07778-8

Self-Help & Relationships

Beating Sugar Addiction
For Dummies
978-1-118-54645-1

Meditation For Dummies,
3rd Edition
978-1-118-29144-3

Seniors

Laptops For Seniors
For Dummies, 3rd Edition
978-1-118-71105-7

Computers For Seniors
For Dummies, 3rd Edition
978-1-118-11553-4

iPad For Seniors For Dummies,
6th Edition
978-1-118-72826-0

Social Security For Dummies
978-1-118-20573-0

Smartphones & Tablets

Android Phones For Dummies,
2nd Edition
978-1-118-72030-1

Nexus Tablets For Dummies
978-1-118-77243-0

Samsung Galaxy S 4
For Dummies
978-1-118-64222-1

Samsung Galaxy Tabs
For Dummies
978-1-118-77294-2

Test Prep

ACT For Dummies, 5th Edition
978-1-118-01259-8

ASVAB For Dummies, 3rd Edition
978-0-470-63760-9

GRE For Dummies, 7th Edition
978-0-470-88921-3

Officer Candidate Tests
For Dummies
978-0-470-59876-4

Physician's Assistant Exam
For Dummies
978-1-118-11556-5

Series 7 Exam For Dummies
978-0-470-09932-2

Windows 8

Windows 8.1 All-in-One
For Dummies
978-1-118-82087-2

Windows 8.1 For Dummies
978-1-118-82121-3

Windows 8.1 For Dummies, Book
+ DVD Bundle
978-1-118-82107-7

Available in print and e-book formats.

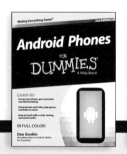
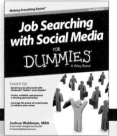

Available wherever books are sold.

For more information or to order direct visit www.dummies.com

Take Dummies with you everywhere you go!

Whether you are excited about e-books, want more from the web, must have your mobile apps, or are swept up in social media, Dummies makes everything easier.

For Dummies is the global leader in the reference category and one of the most trusted and highly regarded brands in the world. No longer just focused on books, customers now have access to the For Dummies content they need in the format they want. Let us help you develop a solution that will fit your brand and help you connect with your customers.

Advertising & Sponsorships

Connect with an engaged audience on a powerful multimedia site, and position your message alongside expert how-to content.

Targeted ads • Video • Email marketing • Microsites • Sweepstakes sponsorship

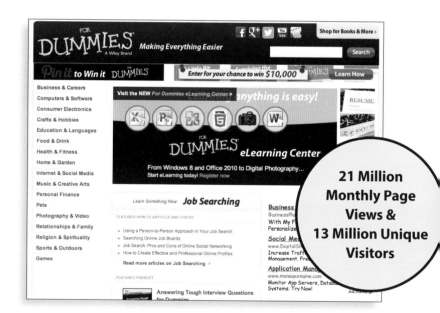

# of For Dummies

Custom Publishing

Reach a global audience in any language by creating a solution that will differentiate you from competitors, amplify your message, and encourage customers to make a buying decision.

Apps • Books • eBooks • Video • Audio • Webinars

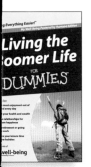

Brand Licensing & Content

Leverage the strength of the world's most popular reference brand to reach new audiences and channels of distribution.

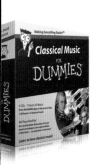

For more information, visit www.Dummies.com/biz

Dummies products make life easier!

- DIY
- Consumer Electronics
- Crafts
- Software
- Cookware
- Hobbies
- Videos
- Music
- Games
- and More!

For more information, go to **Dummies.com** and search the store by category.

FOR
DUMMIE.

A Wiley Bra